Cooperative Learning & Language Arts

Jeanne Stone
In consultation with Dr. Spencer Kagan

Kagan

Kagan

Kagan Publishing
P.O. Box 72008
San Clemente, CA 92673-2008
1(800) 933-2667
www.KaganOnline.com

ISBN: 978-1-879097-13-1

Table of Contents

Part I

An Integrated Language Arts Program ... 1

Part II

Cooperative Learning Structures & Lesson Designs ... 17

Part III

Multi-Structural Lessons ... 97

Table of Structures

Jeanne Stone: *Cooperative Learning & Language Arts: A Multi-Structural Approach*
Kagan Publishing • 1 (800) 933-2667 • www.KaganOnline.com

II

Table of Structures

Foreword
by Spencer Kagan, Ph.D.

Cooperative Learning and Language Arts: A Multi-Structural Approach represents a major step forward in each of two fields: cooperative learning and language arts instruction. By taking a multi-structural approach, the lessons provided tap the full power of cooperative learning and reveal its power to realize the highest goals of the new California State English-Language Arts framework. It is a natural marriage of two fields. Those versed in the goals of the new Framework will find here a powerful set of tools and a practical method for its implementation. Those familiar with the structural approach to cooperative learning will find exciting ways to combine structures to ensure all aspects of the framework are realized.

This book is a major step for instruction in language arts not just because it provides extremely rich lessons which have been extensively field-tested and refined. It does more. It provides a new framework for thinking about an integrated language arts lesson. With a new emphasis on listening and speaking as well as reading and writing, it is impossible to imagine a full implementation of the Framework without cooperative learning.

An Advance for Reading Instruction

Reading separated from listening, speaking, and writing has always suffered. There are three main problems with the traditional approach to reading: (1) Status issues. A negative self-esteem is associated with being assigned to the low reading group. (No matter what we

Jeanne Stone: *Cooperative Learning & Language Arts: A Multi-Structural Approach*
Kagan Publishing • 1 (800) 933-2667 • www.KaganOnline.com

v

call them, the traditional reading groups have always had three names: The Eagles, the Sea Gulls, and the Droppings.) (2) Lack of time. Roundrobin reading in large reading groups can never give students enough time for oral reading. If we have one student at a time reading, and if we divide the reading instruction equally among students, using traditional reading groups, in a class of thirty students each student receives less than two minutes of oral reading per hour. As the Framework indicates, students learn to read by reading, and two minutes an hour will never add up to fluency for many students. (3) Lack of meaningful links. Traditionally, students have spent reading time decoding material with little or no personal meaning.

All three of these problems are elegantly solved with the cooperative approach. As students read in pairs and small groups, there is a disintegration of the status hierarchy and more time per individual student. Further, as they discuss, negotiate, and relate to the reading material through a range of structures such as RoundTable and Team Interviews, they establish the meaningful links — both through what they say and what they hear from peers.

When reading out loud is no longer a separate activity, but included as part of prewriting, revising, and postwriting, as well as across the curriculum in other areas, the cooperative approach leads to much greater time for and love of reading.

An Advance for Listening and Speaking Instruction

Much energy in a traditional classroom is directed toward getting students not to talk. The consequence for many students is not only alienation and a dislike for school, but poor listening and speaking skills. Only when listening and speaking are brought into the curriculum can we improve those skills.

The traditional format is worse than a wasteland with regard to opportunities to improve listening and speaking skills. A traditional approach has never held students accountable for listening skills, and the formally structured speaking opportunities often have been limited to one student addressing a whole class in the form of a book report, "current event," or "sharing time." But children are not born orators, and the thought of addressing the whole class is nothing short of terrifying for many. How refreshing to find throughout Jeanne's book the repeated use of Line-Ups, RoundRobins, Similarity Grouping, Team Interviews, Three-Step Interviews, and Group Discussions to foster both listening and speaking skills in a supportive peer environment.

An Advance for Writing Instruction

The strongest contribution of Jeanne's book is integrating what we know about the writing process with what we know about teaching each of the types of writing, and then providing lessons which integrate both of these methodologies with all four aspects of language arts. The lessons which result have been extensively tested and lead to defined writing skills across the range of objectives, and an increased love of writing for students.

The lessons designed by Jeanne Stone are based on the philosophy that there is often an inverse ratio between teacher talk and student learning and that the teacher best promotes learning by

Foreword

structuring active experiences for the students. The lessons are models of how to increase learning by teaching not through words, but through well-orchestrated experiences.

An Advance for Cooperative Learning

This book also represents a major step for cooperative learning. About ten years ago when I started training teachers in cooperative learning, a typical training session consisted of first demonstrating in a workshop and then in a classroom the power of a cooperative learning structure. I would train teachers in Jigsaw, or in STAD, or in the Color-Coded Co-op Cards. It was as if the teacher's main job was to choose among structures.

As we all became more familiar with what each structure could and could not efficiently accomplish, it became clear that to reach the goals of most lessons, a teacher needed more than one structure. The question became not which cooperative learning structure to use, but rather how to combine various structures to design the most powerful lesson.

My own work therefore shifted. The concept of "Domains of Usefulness" — when to use which structure — became central to the structural approach. The concept of a multi-structural lesson soon followed. It became clear that a teacher versed in a variety of structures uses them as building blocks to create powerful lessons in which each structure provides a learning experience upon which a subsequent structure builds.

This book represents the furthest step in the multi-structural approach for language arts instruction and provides a powerful model of the multi-structural approach to be emulated in all areas. Through these model multi-structural, integrated language arts lessons we view a whole new concept of a lesson — and take another step on a path which is leading to a refreshing redefinition of the teaching process.

Dr. Spencer Kagan

Foreword

Introduction &
Acknowledgements

Introduction

Cooperative Learning and Language Arts: A Multi-Structural Approach is written as a supplement to *Cooperative Learning* by Spencer Kagan, Ph.D. The lessons described in this book are based on the structural approach to cooperative learning. Teachers who have had training in the structural approach may find it easier to implement and visualize the lessons in this book.

California's English-Language Arts Framework calls for an "integrated, literature-based curriculum" that is accessible to all students. Students are to be provided "a myriad of listening, speaking, reading and writing experiences," to help them become "informed and responsible citizens, competent and successful members of the work force, and thinking, fulfilled individuals within society." Cooperative learning provides an arena for students to interact with each other about meaningful content, to work cooperatively on presentations and projects and to take an active role in their own learning.

This guidebook facilitates access to many of the features that are the basis of an effective English-Language Arts program. As members of heterogeneous teams, students work through various cooperative learning structures to make the materials accessible to all students. All of the lessons are integrated, incorporating listening, speaking, reading and writing. Many of the lessons are literature-based, or can be related to literature being used in the classroom. Real life issues are explored. Language skills are taught

Jeanne Stone: *Cooperative Learning & Language Arts: A Multi-Structural Approach*
Kagan Publishing • 1 (800) 933-2667 • www.KaganOnline.com

IX

within the meaningful context of the lesson. All of the lessons feature the writing process. Students have the opportunity to experience many different listening and speaking activities in small group and whole-class settings.

Each multi-structural lesson encompasses one of the four domains of writing: Sensory/Descriptive, Imaginative/ Narrative, Practical/ Informative, and Analytical/ Expository, and can be used at a variety of grade levels.

Part I addresses **an integrated language arts program**. It briefly describes each element — listening, speaking, reading and writing — and provides specific examples for using cooperative learning to develop these skills in the students.

Part II briefly describes each **cooperative learning structure** which is used in the lessons. Ideas for using each structure within a language arts curriculum are presented. The ideas can be used in isolation, as a sponge activity, or as a opening in a teacher-directed lesson.

Part III provides detailed **multi-structural lesson plans** with specific academic outcomes in language arts. The goal is to provide a way for teachers to use cooperative learning as an instructional technique in implementing an integrated language arts curriculum. It is hoped that these lessons will not be an end unto themselves, but will initiate the thought process and become a springboard for teachers in creating their own multi-structural lessons in language arts.

Some of the components for the successful implementation of cooperative learning in the classroom are not addressed in detail in this book. Classroom management, social skills, team formation, and the overall rationale for cooperative learning are described in the book *Cooperative Learning* by Spencer Kagan, Ph.D. It is highly recommended that teachers become well versed and experienced in these aspects of cooperative learning in order to enhance the implementation of this resource book.

Acknowledgements

This second edition could not have been possible without the support and encouragement of many people. As with the first edition, **Spencer Kagan** and the talented staff at Kagan Cooerative Learning prpovided invaluable support through all stages of publishing. Specifically, **Catherine Hurlbert** for her outstanding efforts in reformatting and **Celso Rodriguez** for the development of such wonderful illustrations.

My husband **Ken,** and my sons **Michael, Andrew, and Daniel**, supported me as I worked at all possible moments to complete this second edition.

Hopefully through the use of these lessons, teachers and their classes can find a love of language and expression. May these lessons provide the impetus for teachers to create their own multi-structural lessons to motivate students to listen, speak, read and write.

Intro/Acknowledge

Jeanne Stone: *Cooperative Learning & Language Arts: A Multi-Structural Approach*
X   Kagan Publishing • 1 (800) 933-2667 • www.KaganOnline.com

An Integrated Language Arts Program

Integrating language arts significantly enhances students' learning. Students develop simultaneously as listeners, speakers, readers, and writers as teachers integrate the instruction of these skills.

Cooperative learning can be used effectively as a tool to integrate a language arts program. This chapter gives a brief description of how the four elements of an integrated language arts program, Listening, Speaking, Reading and Writing, are facilitated by cooperative learning structures. The multi-structural lessons in Part III will show how all four elements can be integrated into a lesson.

The following chart summarizes how the cooperative learning structures discussed in this book can be used in an integrated language arts program. The structures that directly involve the language arts processes of listening, speaking, reading or writing are marked with a "O." Those structures that indirectly involve the use of these processes are marked with an "X."

Listening

Most information people acquire is  received aurally. Students need to develop the skills of listening critically and creatively to be able to communicate with each other. Cooperative learning provides a natural vehicle for students to develop these listening skills. Cooperative learning structures that emphasize listen-

Cooperative Learning Structures and Language Arts

	Listening	Speaking	Reading	Writing
Brainstorming	X	O	X	X
Categorizing	O	O	X	X
Co-op Co-op	O	O	O	O
Corners	O	O	X	X
Formations	O	O	X	X
Group Discussion	O	O	X	X
Inside-Outside Circle	O	O	X	X
Jigsaw	O	O	O	O
Line-Ups/Value Lines	O	O	X	X
Numbered Heads Together	O	O	X	X
Paired Reading	X	O	O	X
Paraphrase Passport	O	O		
Partners	O	O	O	O
RoundTable/RoundRobin	O	O	X	O
Similarity Groups	O	O	X	X
Simple Projects	X	X	X	O
Simultaneous Sharing	X	O	O	O
Talking Chips	X	O		
Team Interview	O	O	X	X
Three-Step Interview	O	O	X	X
Word-Webbing	X	X	O	O

ing are Group Discussion, RoundRobin, and Three-Step Interview.

Group Discussion. During Group Discussion, a "tack-on" skill game, Paraphrase Passport, may be added to encourage students to carefully listen to what others are saying. In Paraphrase Passport, a student may only speak after he or she has correctly paraphrased the person who has just spoken. This encourages students to listen, in order to have a chance to speak.

RoundRobin. During RoundRobin, students must listen to the responses other teammates are making, so that they do not repeat the same response. RoundRobin storytelling requires each student to add a sentence or two to the story that is being told around the team. The story can be totally random, or the teacher can provide some direction to incorporate a theme being studied. For example, if students are studying sound, each team can be provided with eight sound cards (crash, bang, boom, crunch, splat, etc.). Each team member takes two cards and must incor-

Part I

Jeanne Stone: *Cooperative Learning & Language Arts: A Multi-Structural Approach*
Kagan Publishing • 1 (800) 933-2667 • www.KaganOnline.com

porate one of the sounds each time he or she adds to the story.

Three-Step Interview. In Three-Step Interview, students are required to listen to what their partners are saying, to interact by asking questions, and to paraphrase what their partners say. Without listening, the student will not be able to paraphrase. For example, before reading *Little Women*, have students interview each other about their brothers and sisters.

Speaking

Speaking activities in a classroom occur both informally and formally. These activities lead to the development of skills that students will need as they become members of the work force. Cooperative learning provides a natural vehicle for students to develop speaking skills. Some examples of cooperative learning structures that emphasize speaking are Corners, Group Discussion, and Think-Pair-Share.

Corners. During Corners students have the opportunity to share their opinions and feelings about a choice they have made. First, they share with someone who has similar opinions and feelings. Students then hear what others think and feel, which gives them an opportunity to accept and value individual differences. For example, after reading the story *Charlotte's Web* by E. B. White, students select the character that they most identify with — Templeton, Fern, Wilbur, or Charlotte, meet with others who have the same favorite character, and share

reasons why they identify with that character. The groups then share from corner to corner.

Group Discussion. During a Group Discussion, students listen and respond to the comments of their teammates. Group Discussion topics may involve sharing opinions about a character, discussing a character's motives, or discussing what might happen next in the story or book.

Think-Pair-Share. Before students speak, it is important to provide some think time. Think-Pair-Share allows students to think about an answer, rehearse a response with a partner, and then participate in some kind of whole-class sharing. For example, during the reading of a story, the teacher stops to have students guess what will happen next. The students think about it, share their ideas with a partner, and then share them with the whole class.

Reading

Students learn to read by reading. By interacting with literature, students can become motivated to read, and as they read, develop the necessary skills to get the most out of what they read. Cooperative learning structures can be used to prepare students for reading by helping them to relate prior experiences to the theme, to make predictions about the text, to get the most from the text when reading, and to respond to the text they read. Some cooperative learning structures that can be used in reading are Paired Reading, RoundTable or RoundRobin, Team Interview, and Think-Pair-Share.

Part I

Paired Reading. To make the reading content accessible to all, students can participate in Paired Reading. Two students read together, alternating sentences, paragraphs, or pages depending on the length of the book.

RoundTable. Students are able to share prior experiences that relate to the theme being studied. If they have a limited experience with the theme, they can be enriched by the answers the other team members are giving. For example, if the students are to explore the idea of friendship, they could RoundTable or RoundRobin words that describe a friend.

Team Interview. To help students actively respond to a piece of literature they read, have them take on the roles of the characters, and be interviewed in their roles. After deciding which role each team member will have, one at a time, each student sits in the "hot seat" in the center of the team. The other team members ask the student questions which they must answer "in character." For example, following a discussion of bullies, the students do a Paired Reading (or experience the telling) of *The Three Billy Goats Gruff.* Each student selects the character he or she wishes to portray, the small billy goat, the middle-sized billy goat, the large billy goat or the troll. Team members begin asking questions of the "small billy goat." The students then continue to interview each character in turn.

Think-Pair-Share. To help students get meaning from text, they need to develop comprehension skills. An important way to help students achieve reading comprehension is to show them how to sample, predict, and confirm. Before students begin reading, have them study the cover of the book or an opening picture. Ask them to think what the book will be about. Have them share with a partner. Quickly collect different predictions from the class and record them to compare after reading into the story. At different times during a story, whether it is being read to the students or they are reading it, the students should be stopped, to predict what they think might be happening next. During the reading of *Harry and the Lady Next-Door* by Gene Zion, stop several times to have students predict the success of Harry's latest plan for silencing the lady next-door.

Writing

 Writing as a process can be defined as the complex system people use when transcribing ideas into written form. This writing process is made up of seven interrelated stages:

1. *Prewriting*
2. *Writing*
3. *Responding*
4. *Revising*
5. *Editing*
6. *Evaluating*
7. *Postwriting*

These stages occur recursively rather than sequentially. For example, as students begin to formulate ideas during prewriting, they may ask for responses from other students rather than wait until their writings are finished. Students may edit as they are writing, and then edit again later after their writing is finished. It should

<u>**Part I**</u>

also be noted that not all writing assignments require that students go through each stage of the writing process.

The relationship between each of these seven stages and the cooperative learning structures is presented in the box below.

The multi-structural language arts lessons in Part III generally follow the stages of the writing process as listed on the previous page. However, not every lesson will encompass each stage in the writing process. The lessons are designed to focus on skill development in specific stages. Some lessons will concentrate more on the prewriting stage, while others may concentrate on the responding or editing stages.

Teacher's Note: For teachers using a Writing Workshop in their classrooms, the multi-structural lessons in this book may be too structured and too lengthy. Some ideas on how these lessons can be integrated into a Writing Workshop are:

- Use part of the multi-structural lesson, or one of the ideas from the structure descriptions, to "teach" a mini-lesson.
- Allow students to choose the direction their writing will go after the prewriting experience in the multi-structural lessons rather than assigning the given topic.
- Use a multi-structural lesson as a whole class activity at key times throughout the school year.
- Use multi-structural lessons to expose the students to literature that they can emulate in their own writing.
- Focus on the listening, speaking, and reading aspects of the lessons.

Cooperative Learning Structures and the Writing Process

	Prewriting	Writing	Responding	Revising	Editing	Evaluating	Postwriting
Brainstorming	X						
Categorizing	O						
Co-op Co-op	O	O	O	O	O	O	O
Corners	O						
Formations	O						
Group Discussion	O	O	O		O	O	
Inside-Outside Circle	O		O				
Jigsaw	O	O	O	O	O		O
Line-Ups/Value Lines	O					O	
Numbered Heads Together					O		
Partners	O	O	O	O	O		O
RoundTable/RoundRobin	O	O	O		O		
Send-A-Problem	O				O		
Similarity Groups	O						
Think-Pair-Share	O		O	O		O	
Three-Step Interview	O	O	O			O	
Word-Webbing	O						

Part I

Stage 1. Prewriting

Prewriting, the first stage in the writing process, is any experience or activity that motivates a person to write. Prewriting uses a variety of active experiences to expand the ideas writers have and to help them organize their ideas before they begin to write. Oral storytelling, role playing, art, field trips, interviews, guided imagery, and literature are examples of the experiences that can be used for pre-writing. It is important to show students that they have something to say, and to move them from just thinking about it to writing about it.

A variety of cooperative learning structures can be used to enhance Prewriting experiences. Some examples are Round-table, RoundRobin, Line-ups, Value Lines, Corners, Similarity Grouping, Three-Step Interview, and Brainstorming.

RoundTable and *RoundRobin.*

Students contribute to a list of ideas that are relevant to the writing topic. This list helps the students become more productive writers. The list can include individual words, phrases, or even whole sentences. For example, after the students have read Jack Prelutsky's poem "I'm Thankful" in *The New Kid on the Block*, they could RoundTable all the things for which they are thankful. Each student could then pick three or four things from the list that they would include in a poem of their own.

The main benefit of RoundTable is that all students use their diverse backgrounds to add to the list. Those who may have a more limited background on the topic are enriched, and aided, by those with a more thorough background. As the topics change, so

do the strengths on the team. Using Simultaneous RoundTable, each student can collect information for a particular topic of interest to him or her. Each student writes his or her topic on the top of a page, as the papers rotate, the students add their ideas to their team-mates' topics.

RoundTable and RoundRobin can also be used to begin writing and organizing ideas. Using Simultaneous RoundTable each student begins a story on a different piece of paper. As the papers are passed, the other students on the team add sentences to the stories.

Line-ups and *Value Lines.*

Students have an opportunity to meet and discuss topics with others who have similar or diverse views. For example, if students have just finished reading *Harriet the Spy* by Louise Fitzhugh, they could form a Value Line on whether or not they agree or disagree with the fact that Harriet's journal should remain a secret, only for her eyes, or should be open to be read by anyone. By folding the value line, those who feel it should be secret, and those who feel it should not be, can form a team. The teams discuss their respective points of view, before beginning to address the issue in writing.

Corners and *Similarity Groups.*

Students meet with others who have a similar interest, as well as to hear other points of view. For example, after reading a book, the students select their favorite character and join that group. By sharing within groups, the students begin to identify the characteristics of their favorite character. By paraphrasing across groups, students can see different points of view about the other charac-

Part I

Jeanne Stone: *Cooperative Learning & Language Arts: A Multi-Structural Approach*
Kagan Publishing • 1 (800) 933-2667 • www.KaganOnline.com

ters. The students from the same corners or similarity groups can meet to delve into the book, as seen from their character's point of view, as a precursor to rewriting part of the book or extending the book, using the voice of their character.

Group Discussion. Students create and exchange unique ideas to different low consensus topics. Students discuss their ideas in either a structured (Talking Chips) or unstructured approach. Following a group discussion, students share their ideas with others. Group Discussion allows students the opportunity to explore and test out ideas before writing. For example, after reading the book *Bread and Jam for Frances* by Russell Hoban, students share their favorite foods. The discussion continues with students discussing, "What would it be like to eat the same food all day long, for days on end? What would you do if all you had to eat was _____?"

Three-Step Interview. Students have the opportunity to begin formalizing their ideas by sharing them with another person. During Three-Step Interview students are also exposed to the different ideas expressed by their teammates. This may move their thinking in a different direction than they had previously thought. For example, before students read *Ira Sleeps Over* by Bernard Waber, have them interview each other about spending the night at a friend's house. This helps them remember the feelings and thoughts they had when they were going to spend a night at a friend's house, preparing them to write a letter to Ira telling him whether or not he can bring his teddy bear.

Brainstorming. This is a quick way of making a list of ideas to work with when writing. Usually, once the ideas are brainstormed, they are categorized. (To aid in categorizing, it is important that each idea be written on a separate piece of paper.) Categorizing organizes the ideas and starts to set a focus for the writing.

For example, having read *The Story of My Life* by Helen Keller, students brainstorm all the important events they can remember in Helen Keller's life. The events are then categorized in any way that is important to the team. Some may categorize them by time periods, others by the people involved (Helen herself, family, friends, etc.). This categorized list then becomes the organizational flow for the writing that follows.

Stage 2. Writing

Writing is the stage in the writing process when ideas are recorded on paper. The focus in writing is for the students to write fluently, expressing their ideas quickly with little concern for correctness. Students need to understand that the first draft is for synthesizing thoughts and ideas from the prewriting experience, that the paper can be messy and have errors. Skipping lines when writing the first draft, gives students the room to work on revisions later. Students need to be given frequent opportunities to do all kinds of writing, to write for different audiences, and to have a specific purpose for their writing. Fastwrite (freewriting) helps students write fluently, because it encourages them to write what they think about the topic without worrying about organization or correctness.

Part I

Cooperative learning structures can help students when developing the skills of writing for an audience (Three-Step Interview, Team Interview) and when setting a specific purpose for the writing (Three-Step Interview, Group Discussion).

Three-Step Interview and **Team Interview.** Students have the opportunity to "practice" their piece of writing with the audience. During the interview, students can listen and ask questions as if they were the intended audience (a parent, a newspaper subscriber, a congressman). For example, students select their favorite character from a book or story. They create a setting for their character that is foreign to the character (Thomas Jefferson at a T.V. press conference). The other students in the group can become members of the foreign setting and ask questions of the character.

Group Discussion. Students explore low consensus issues and share their responses with the class. For example, students may explore the different purposes an author had for writing a particular poem, essay, story or book. Students can also look at a writing assignment, decide on its purpose, and discuss the different ways for approaching the writing.

Stage 3. Responding

Responding allows students to get reactions from other students on what they have written. Responses are quick, first reactions to a piece of writing. The responses are usually given in the form of statements, questions, or suggestions, and can be given orally or in written form. The responses provide guidance to the writers in clarifying their writing. Structuring responding in the classroom can lead to greater student success. Whole-class sharing sessions model for the class what responding is all about by using a piece of student writing on an overhead or on a chart paper. Gambits (open ended, model phrases) can be provided to guide students in making appropriate responses. (See the Gambits for Responding box)

Cooperative learning structures that can be used for responding are RoundRobin, Simultaneous RoundTable, Group Discussion, Inside-Outside Circle, and Three-Step Interview.

RoundRobin. Each student reads his or her piece of writing to the team two times. The other students listen and prepare to respond. After a fifteen to twenty second pause when the reader is finished, the other students, in turn, orally respond to the writing that they heard.

Simultaneous RoundTable. Each team member has three response sheets. The pieces of writing are passed around the team. After reading each writing, the team members write statements, questions, or suggestions on a **Response Sheet** (provided in this chapter.) The RoundTable is completed when the team members have read and responded to the writings from all of their teammates.

Group Discussion. This structure is similar to RoundRobin, but the team is not limited to making their responses in turn around the team. Group Discussion allows the students to discuss favorite parts of the writing and discuss ways the writing might be revised.

Part I

Inside-Outside Circle. This is a brief way to share writing. Rather than sharing whole pieces of writing (unless they are short stories or poems), the students only share a select part, one they especially like, or one to which they especially want responses.

Three-Step Interview. Students share their writing with a partner, and then hear how the partner summarizes the writing to the other teammates. This allows the author an inside look at how his or her writing is perceived by others.

Stage 4. Revising

In the Revising stage, students "resee" their writings in light of the comments received from the other students. This is a time for students to add to, delete, and/or change the ideas in their writing, but not correct it! Throughout the Writing Process, students continually reread and make small changes. Now that the writing is finished, students look at the writing as a whole and answer such questions as, "Does it say what I want it to say? Did people understand what I wanted them to "see?" Do I need to add more details? Does it communicate to the correct audience? Does it successfully meet its purpose?" Students need to be guided in developing techniques that allow them to address ideas such as organization, sentence structure (sentence combining and sentence expansion), word choice, clarity, and emphasis. Remember though that not all pieces of writing need to be taken through the revision stage.

Cooperative learning structures that can be helpful in Revising are Think-Pair-Share and Jigsaw.

Think-Pair-Share. During revising students rethink something they have written and get immediate feedback from an audience. For example, during responding, students have asked questions about the house in a teammate's story. The student can think about a way to add to the description and share it with a teammate to see if it clarifies the questions.

Jigsaw. Each member of the team becomes a resource during revising. For example, each student of the team becomes responsible for a particular strategy used in revising — sentence combining, sentence expansion, show not tell and organization. After learning about the strategy, the team members can tutor each other on how to use the strategies in their writings.

Gambits for Responding

Pointing

I like the part when you said ...
I liked the words ...
... and ... stuck in my mind after you finished reading your writing.
I didn't understand ...
I wanted to know more about ...

Summarizing

I think the main point of your writing is ...
To me your story says ...
To me the word ..., summarizes your writing.

Telling

When you said ..., it made me think of ...
I felt ... when you read your story.
I wondered ... when you said ...
I saw ... in my mind when you were reading ... part of your writing.

Part I

Response Sheet

What did you like best about this paper? What made it hold your attention?

_____
_____
_____
_____
_____

What questions do you have? What is confusing or unclear to you?

_____
_____
_____
_____
_____
_____

What would you like know more about? What needs more detail?

_____
_____
_____
_____
_____
_____

How would you rate this story on a scale of 1 (low) to 4 (high)? If you give a rating of 1 or 2 tell what you think would make the story better.

_____
_____
_____
_____
_____
_____

Part I

Jeanne Stone: *Cooperative Learning & Language Arts: A Multi-Structural Approach*
Kagan Publishing • 1 (800) 933-2667 • www.KaganOnline.com

Stage 5. Editing

Editing is the stage of the writing process in which the students begin to look at correctness. The content of the writing is set and now the students look at the mechanics (spelling, grammar, punctuation, capitalization), diction (precise word choices), syntax (sentence structure), accuracy of the text, proper manuscript form (title, heading), and proofreading (to make sure what was said is what the writer wants to say). It is during editing that specific lessons on mechanics and grammar can be taught. The best time to teach students the conventions of writing is as they need them in their writing.

Students can work cooperatively to edit their work and provide support for each other. Not all editing should be done in a cooperative manner as it is very important for students to learn to independently edit their own writing. Cooperative learning structures that can be used for Editing are Numbered Heads Together, Simultaneous RoundTable, and Partner Editing.

Numbered Heads Together.

As students enter the editing stage of the writing process, the teacher can use direct instruction to teach any necessary conventions that the students might need. After the direct instruction, the teacher can use Numbered Heads Together to check for understanding, and to help develop mastery of the specific mechanics or grammar skill being taught.

Simultaneous RoundTable.

Each round focuses on a specific mechanics or grammar issue. In each round, the students pass their papers around the team so they are checked three other times for the particular errors. For example, if the students had completed writing and revising a letter to persuade their parents to let them do something they usually can't do, the rounds for Simultaneous RoundTable might be:

Round 1: Letter format (date, greeting, closing)
Round 2: Mechanics (punctuation and capitalization with an emphasis on commas)
Round 3: Use of effective, persuasive language
Round 4: Sentence structure

Partner Editing.

Students edit their own writing while being coached by a teammate. After the students have been trained in editing their papers, they work through each round twice. Partner 1 reads for errors while Partner 2 coaches, then Partner 2 reads while Partner 1 coaches.

Stage 6. Evaluating

Evaluating is the part of the writing process that generally receives the most focus, though it is only part of the post-writing activities. It is important to help students see evaluation only as a part of the whole writing process. Evaluation should be used to support student writing and promote growth in it. In order to do this, students must be aware before writing, if, how, and by whom they will be evaluated. A wide variety of methods should be used in evaluating student writing. Evaluation of student writing samples should be based on set criteria that support the reason for the assessment. Students can be trained to evaluate their own and other students' writings.

Some of the different forms of Evaluation are primary trait scoring, holistic scoring, and analytic scoring. **Primary trait scoring** focuses on the special features a piece of writing has in regard to the

<u>*Part I*</u>

audience, the purpose, and the subject. For example, if a student was writing to explain how to assemble a bicycle, one of the primary traits would be sequential organization. Another might be clearness of language when describing the parts of the bicycle.

Holistic scoring looks at the piece of writing as a whole and assesses its ability to communicate to the reader. It can assess the papers by matching them to similar papers, by assigning each paper a numerical score, or by scoring the paper's prominent features. Holistic scoring can be used to quickly assess large numbers of papers.

Analytic scoring identifies the specific needs in a piece of student writing. A list is made of the prominent features that should appear in the piece of writing, and the writing is evaluated according to the list. For example, for a writing sample that asked the students to write the directions for assembling a peanut butter and jelly sandwich, the analytic scoring guide might have such things as clear and concise description, sequential organization, variety of sentence types, correct punctuation and capitalization, and spelling.

A sample scoring guide of each type is included in the Scoring Guides handouts.

Objective tests can measure the grasp of the conventions (and therefore editing skills).

Some cooperative learning structures that can be used for evaluating are Group Discussion and Think-Pair-Share.

Group Discussion. Once students have become familiar with the particular scoring system being used, the students can use a scoring guide to score a set of papers. For example, the teacher has provided the class with a holistic scoring guide and some model student papers. The teacher leads the class through reading each paper, assigning it a score, and discussing any discrepancies in the scores the students assign. The students can then look at their team's papers (or those of another team) for scoring. Each student reads a paper and assigns it a score. After reading all the papers, the students compare scores, discuss any discrepancies and come to a consensus score.

Think-Pair-Share. After students are comfortable with the scoring system being used, Think-Pair-Share can be used for students to score a paper and compare it with another student's interpretation before sharing his or her score with the class. For example, the students are familiar with the primary trait scoring guide being used for the particular assignment. Each student has received copies of the papers that are being assessed. The teacher tells all students to read Paper #1 and think about the appropriate score. Students share this score with a partner as well as any reasons for the particular score. If the scores agree, the students can continue on. If there is a question with a score, the students can consult with the teacher or with their teammates.

Stage 7. Postwriting

Postwriting is all the activities that can be done with a finished piece of writing. It provides students the opportunity to see that writing is not only for the teacher's eyes. The writing can be charted, posted, illustrated, mailed, included in a newspaper or a magazine, or numerous other alternatives. Cooperative learning

Part I

Jeanne Stone: *Cooperative Learning & Language Arts: A Multi-Structural Approach*
Kagan Publishing • 1 (800) 933-2667 • www.KaganOnline.com

Scoring Guides
Holistic Scoring Guide
Imaginative/Narrative

Score of

- Specific details describe the setting and the characters. The reader becomes involved with the story.
- There is a clear plan of organization. All events are sequenced and connected to the story line.
- There is an excellent command of language structure and vocabulary.
- There is an excellent grasp of spelling and mechanics. The reader is not slowed by having to decipher handwriting, spelling, or sentence structure.

Score of

- Setting and characters are included in the story, but are not fully described. The reader has a few questions about the story.
- Sequence is used to organize the story. Some events are not connected to the story theme.
- There is an adequate command of language structure and vocabulary.
- There is an adequate grasp of spelling and mechanics. The errors do not confuse the reader.

Score of

- Details and imagination are lacking.
- There is no plan of organization. Irrelevant events are incorporated into the story.
- There is a lack of command of language structure and vocabulary. The reader must frequently reread to understand the ideas the student is presenting.
- There is a lack of sufficient grasp of spelling and mechanics to communicate with the reader.

Part I

Scoring Guides
Analytical Scoring Guide
Imaginative/Narrative

	High	Middle	Low
Content			
Ideas	Uses details to describe the setting and characters. Writes to hold the interest of the reader. Includes original ideas.	Writer includes setting and characters but does not describe them. Writer does not hold the reader's interest.	Writer does not include details. Shows very little imagination.
Organization	Clear plan of organization. Uses sequence in telling about events. All events are connected to the story line.	Most events are in sequence. Some events are not connected to the story line.	Doesn't sequence events. Adds many irrelevant details.
Mechanics			
Syntax	Sentences are clear. Occasional run-ons and few fragments, if any. Uses a variety of sentence types.	Sentences are basically clear. Requires occasional rereading of a sentence. Some run-ons and fragments.	Reader has difficulty understanding sentences. Many run-ons and fragments. Omits words or sentence parts.
Usage/ Word Choice	Uses standard English (subject-verb agreement, personal pronouns, present and past tense).	Some errors in standard English.	Many errors in standard English.
Punctuation Capitalization	Begins and ends sentences correctly. Uses commas and apostrophes where needed. Uses capital letters where needed.	Some errors in punctuation and capitalization.	Lacks understanding of what to punctuate and capitalize.
Spelling	High frequency words are spelled correctly most of the time. Misspelled words are close to the actual spelling.	May misspell high frequency words. Some phonetic spelling.	Many misspellings.

Part I

Scoring Guides
Primary/Secondary Trait Scoring Guide

Prompt: Think of all the things you like. Write a poem using descriptive words that list the different things you like.

Primary Trait Scoring Guide

Score   *Description*

 This poem creates pictures for the reader. It uses descriptive language in highlighting the things that are special to the writer.

 This poem uses some descriptive language. The reader has some feeling of what is special to the writer.

 This poem is merely a list of things.

Secondary Trait Scoring Guide

Score   *Description*

 This poem is neat and easy to read. It has fewer than three errors in capitalization, punctuation and/or spelling.

 This poem is not as neat and easy to read. It has three to five errors in capitalization, punctuation, and/or spelling.

 This poem is not neat and easy to read. There are many errors in capitalization, punctuation, and/or spelling.

Part I

structures that can be used in publishing writing are Co-op Co-op, Jigsaw, Teams Tour, and Roam the Room.

Co-op Co-op. When students have completed their writings, as a team they can decide what format would best fit the writings — magazine, newspaper, or book. The students discuss what they need to know to produce the finished project and who will take responsibility for each part. The students prepare their individual sections, and then synthesize the sections into the final team project. The team projects are then presented to the class as a whole. For example, if the team decided to create a magazine, they could decide that the responsibilities on the project might be format, cover and art work, circulation, and printing. Each student would collect the information on their particular responsibility and then, through joint effort, the magazine would actually be published.

Jigsaw. In Jigsaw, each student would learn about one aspect of completing the team project and then take that information back to the team. For example, if each team was to create a book. One student from each team may learn about binding, one about table of contents, one about cover illustration, and one about the title page.

Teams Tour and **Roam-the-Room.** Teams Tour and Roam-the-Room are two ways of simultaneous sharing that adapt well to sharing finished pieces of writing. In Teams Tour, the teams travel to different teams to have the finished "product" shared. In Roam-the-Room, the finished "products" are mounted in the classroom and the teams can wander through the room looking at the "products" before returning to their seats to compare notes.

Part I

Jeanne Stone: *Cooperative Learning & Language Arts: A Multi-Structural Approach*
Kagan Publishing • 1 (800) 933-2667 • www.KaganOnline.com

Cooperative Learning Structures and Lesson Designs

The following section identifies each of the cooperative learning structures used in this book. Each structure contains a brief description, the steps to follow, any variations and/or cautions, and ideas specific to language arts.

The brief description gives an overview of the structure and its usefulness in the classroom. The structures can be grouped according to their Domains of Usefulness: Classbuilding, Teambuilding, Thinking Skills, Mastery, Information Sharing, Writing, Cooperative Project Designs, and Division of Labor Designs.

Classbuilding

Classbuilding structures promote networking among all the students in a class and create a positive context in which teams can learn. Classbuilding structures used in this book are:

Corners
Formations
Inside-Outside Circle
Line-Ups and Value Lines
Mix-Freeze-Group
Similarity Groups

Teambuilding

Teambuilding structures promote enthusiasm, trust, and mutual support within a team. Strong team spirit and unity can lead to more efficient academic work. Teambuilding structures used in this book are:

Formations
RoundRobin

Jeanne Stone: *Cooperative Learning & Language Arts: A Multi-Structural Approach*
Kagan Publishing • 1 (800) 933-2667 • www.KaganOnline.com

17

RoundTable
Team Interview
Team Projects

Mastery

Mastery structures help students develop skills and mastery of academic content. These structures are useful in dealing with high consensus materials, such as knowledge and comprehension. Mastery structures used in this book are:

Inside-Outside Circle
Numbered Heads Together
RoundRobin
RoundTable

Thinking Skills

Thinking Skills structures provide the opportunity for students to create and exchange unique, novel ideas to low consensus questions. Thinking Skills structures used in this book are:

4S Brainstorming
Sorting
Team Discussion
Team Interview
Think-Pair-Share
Three-Step Interview
Two-Box Induction
Word-Webbing

Information Sharing

It is highly recommended that teachers incorporate information sharing of team and individual ideas and responses as much as possible. Sharing information among teammates enhances teambuilding, tutoring, concept development, and creating positive peer groups. Sharing information among classmates enhances classbuilding as well as higher level thinking skills. A benefit of simultaneous information sharing is the large amount of student involvement and interaction in comparison to the mode of sharing where the teacher calls on one student at a time. Information sharing structures in this book are:

Sharing among Teammates
RoundRobin
Team Interview
Three-Step Interview

Sharing Among Teams
Teams Post
Carbon Share
Class Notebooks
Gallery Tour
One Stray
Roam-the-Room
Stand-N-Share
Teams Consult
Three Stray

Writing

Some activities specifically dealing with writing are included in this chapter. Because they each describe a specific type of student behavior and can be used repeatedly with different content, they are structures. Writing structures in this book are:

Fastwriting
Guided Imagery
Partner Editing

Part II

Cooperative Project Design

Cooperative Projects involve task specialization within and between teams. Each student makes a unique contribution to the team and each team makes a unique contribution to the class. A Cooperative Project design used in this book is:

Co-op Co-op

Division of Labor Designs

Division of Labor Designs have each student make a unique contribution to the task at hand. It creates a strong interdependence among teammates. Division of Labor Designs used in this book are:

Jigsaw
Partners

Included with each structure are the basic steps to follow when using the structure. It is important to preview the steps, so that the teacher understands exactly what the students will be doing. Frequently included in the text of the multi-structural lessons are statements, such as "Have the students RoundTable snacks they like to eat." or "Using Think-Pair-Share have the students share their favorite character." Without a basic understanding of the step-by-step for the structures, the students and the teacher might be uneasy during the lesson. A review of *Cooperative Learning* by Spencer Kagan can provide more detailed information.

Variations or cautions are included for some of the structures. These are special hints that come in handy while using the particular structure. For example, when using Three-Step Interview, it is important to have the students proceed step-by-step through the structure as a class, rather than racing through on their own time schedule.

Part II

Brainstorming

Let's hurry!

Let's think of a silly idea!

Can we add to this idea?

All ideas count!

*You can find **Brainstorming** in Lessons 1, 2, 6, 9, 10, 15, 16, 18, 20, 21, 22, 23.*

Steps

1 The teacher assigns roles based on the 4-S's of Brainstorming. The roles and some things that students might say in the roles are:
- Speed
    "Let's hurry."
    "Quick! More ideas!"
- Suspend Judgement
    "All ideas are great."
    "Another fantastic idea."
- Silly
    "Let's have some crazy ideas."
- Synergy
    "Let's have some ideas like that!"
    "Let's change that to…"

2 The teacher assigns a Recorder who will write each response on a different piece of paper (to facilitate sorting later).

3 The teacher announces the topic and the students begin.

Brainstorming encourages creativity and allows for collecting many possible answers. The team throws out as many ideas as possible while a recorder records each idea on a small piece of paper. An effective form of Brainstorming includes roles being assigned to each team member. The roles correlate to the four S's of Brainstorming.

Speed — work fast, under time pressure, to come up with as many ideas as possible. The team member assigned this role would say such things as, "We only have one minute left. Let's hurry! Let's get quicker with our responses."

Suspend Judgement — no evaluation of ideas. The team member assigned this role would say such things as, "All ideas count. Let's not talk about the ideas now."

Silly — all ideas are relevant and are included. The team member assigned this role would say such things as, "Let's think of some silly ideas."

Synergy — to build on other ideas. The team member assigned this role would say such things as, "What other ideas does that give you? Review the list to help you think of other ideas."

Recorder — to record the ideas as quickly as possible, each idea on a separate piece of paper. Assigning this job to the Speed Captain or the Suspend Judgement Captain facilitates the Brainstorming.

Variations

RoundTable Record
Rather than have only one member on the team be the recorder, have the team RoundTable Record. Using the small pieces of paper in the center of the table each person, in turn, records an idea. Continue for several rounds.

Think-Pad Brainstorming
Rather than placing the paper for recording in the center of the team, each team member is given a set number of pieces of paper. The teacher announces the topic and the number of responses for each round. Each student responds to the topic and puts his or her responses in the center of the team.

Example: Round One, each student writes three adjectives (cold, silent, long). Round Two, each student writes two verb phrases (slides quietly). Round Three, each student writes two prepositional phrases telling where (through the tall grass). After the Think-Pad Brainstorming, all the words are available to the team members as they work to complete the assigned task. (Create a sentence about a snake: The cold, silent snake slides quietly through the tall grass.)

Other Think-Pad Brainstorming topics include: Setting (beach, forest, dungeon), Characters (ten-year old, a person with super powers, a bear), Senses (What do you hear at the beach? Feel? Smell?), A given emotion (What makes you angry? What makes you happy?), etc.

Class Brainstorming
Class Brainstorming allows the whole class to participate in the brainstorming sessions. This is especially helpful in the primary grades when the students are not independent writers. It can be left unstructured so that anyone responds at any time. To help elicit responses from all students, set a series of time periods up with only certain team members responding during those time periods. For example, for the first minute only team member #1's can respond, the second minute only team member #2's, the third minute only team member #3's, and the fourth minute only team member #4's.

Brainstorming

Jeanne Stone: *Cooperative Learning & Language Arts: A Multi-Structural Approach*
Kagan Publishing • 1 (800) 933-2667 • www.KaganOnline.com

Brainstorming
A c t i v i t i e s

Prewriting Activity
Brainstorm as many _____ (animals, characters, settings, problems) as you can.

Rhyming Words
Brainstorm as many rhyming words as you can for _____.

Adjectives
Brainstorm as many adjectives as you can to describe _____.

Prereading Activity
As a prereading experience, have the students brainstorm something related to a story. For example, brainstorm all the things that a train could carry (before *The Little Engine That Could* by Watty Piper).

Compare and Contrast
As a prewriting experience before comparing the city to the country, students can brainstorm everything that is in a city and then everything that is in the country.

Color Words
Brainstorm things that are red, yellow, blue, etc.

Extending the Story
During a tall tale unit, have the students brainstorm about all the things Paul Bunyan and Babe, the blue ox, might be able to do.

Going on a Trip
Brainstorm the things you would take with you on a trip.

Consonant Sounds
Brainstorm as many words as you can that start with the letter "b".

Favorite Foods
Brainstorm foods you like to eat. Use them to prepare a restaurant menu.

Sentence Combining
Brainstorm as many short sentences as you can about Disneyland. These can later be the sentences used in a sentence combining activity.

Co-op Co-op

You can find **Co-op Co-op** *in Lesson 3*

Co-op Co-op is a cooperative project design built around a cooperative team project.

Students work individually within their teams in order to learn something to satisfy their own curiosity about themselves and the world. Each team member then contributes to the completion of a team project that synthesizes the information from all the team members. The final product is shared with the whole class so that other class members may also benefit from the learning. They are cooperating in order to cooperate. The learning is not seen as progress toward a predetermined teacher-defined goal, but as a process that flows out of the interests of the students.

Co-op Co-op lesson design is simple and flexible. The inclusion of certain steps increases the probability of success of the lesson. Each of the steps allows for the use of one or two structures to facilitate the student interaction. When Co-op Co-op is used in the lessons in this book, all ten steps may or may not be included, depending on the nature of the lesson. The ten most essential elements or steps of Co-op Co-op follow.

Steps

1 Student-Centered Class Discussion

Initial experiences, including class discussion, are designed to stimulate student curiosity and identify student interests in topics they wish to explore.

2 Selection of Student Study Teams

This step is usually designed to maximize heterogeneity within teams along the dimensions of ability, sex, and ethnic background. The students may be assigned to teams or may be allowed to select their teams on the basis of their interests.

3 Teambuilding and Skill Development

Teambuilding and cooperative skill development are incorporated to increase within-team cooperation and communication skills.

4 Team Topic Selection

Each team discusses the various topics of interest which were suggested during the class discussion and selects a topic of the most interest to themselves as a team. If two teams choose the same topic, they can be encouraged to reach a compromise, either by dividing the topic or by having one of the teams choose some other topic of interest. Each team will want to make a unique contribution to the class learning goals.

5 Mini-topic Selection

Each team member becomes responsible for one aspect of the team topic. The students decide how to divide the topic and mini-topics are selected by the students; they are subject to teacher approval, but are not assigned.

6 Mini-topic Preparation

Team members individually gather and organize materials on their mini-topics. The preparation may involve library research, surveys, interviews, experimentation, creation of an individual project, introspection, or an expressive activity, such as writing, acting or painting.

7 Mini-topic Presentations

Each student presents to the team what they have learned on their topic. There is usually time for feedback from the team and a second round of presentations designed to respond to the needs of the team.

8 Preparation of Team Presentations

Teams synthesize the material of the mini-topics to prepare their team presentation.

9 Team Presentations

Presentations are made to the whole class. Non-lecture formats are preferred, such as demonstrations, learning centers, skits, debates, and audio-visual presentations.

Co-op Co-op

Jeanne Stone: *Cooperative Learning & Language Arts: A Multi-Structural Approach*
Kagan Publishing • 1 (800) 933-2667 • www.KaganOnline.com

10 Evaluation

Evaluation is made of (1) individual mini-topic presentations to the team (by teammates); (2) team presentations to the whole class (by classmates); and (3) individual papers of projects on mini-topics (by teacher). Students participate in the construction of evaluation forms; they are evaluating the extent to which individuals and teams helped further the class in reaching its learning goals.

Scheduling

Co-op Co-op units can be scheduled in a variety of ways:

- Mini Co-op Co-op projects can be carried out in one day. In this short format, teams take only ten or fifteen minutes to prepare short presentations of five minutes or so.

- A Co-op Co-op unit may run concurrently with a traditional schedule, in which students work one or two days a week on their Co-op Co-op projects, which, in that format, take four or five weeks to prepare.

- An intensive two week Co-op Co-op project at the end of a quarter allows students to extend, reinforce, and integrate the knowledge they have acquired.

Co-op Co-op

Co-op Co-op
A c t i v i t i e s

Publishing Writings
When students have completed their writings, as a team they can decide what format would best fit the writings — magazine, newspaper, or book. The students discuss what they need to know to produce the finished project and who will take responsibility for each part. The students prepare their individual sections and then synthesize the sections into the final team project. The team projects are then presented to the class as a whole. For example, if the team decided to create a magazine, they could decide that the responsibilities on the project might be format, cover and art work, circulation, and printing. Each student would collect the information on their particular responsibility and then, through joint effort, the magazine would actually be published.

Poetry in Depth
Teams can explore four selected works by a particular poet. Each student studies the time period a particular poem was written and the poet's life at that time. The team then compares notes and prepare a presentation that chronicles the life of the poet and how his or her poetry was influenced by the historical events of the time.

Exploring Theme
After selecting a theme to explore, each team member can read a book that deals with the theme. Each member prepares a synopsis of the book to share with his teammates. After the books have been shared, the team begins looking for a way that the books can be presented to the class. The presentation should help the class can see how the books are connected by the theme, the similarities and differences of the books, character traits held by the main characters that are integral to the theme, and other books that are connected with the same theme.

A New Literary Award
After all the teams study the different literary awards that are given out today (for example, the Caldecott Medal and the Newbery Medal), each team creates a new literary award and nominates possible winners.

Legendary Heros and Heroines
Each team selects a hero or heroine from American folktales (such as Paul Bunyan, Pecos Bill, Annie Christmas, Davy Crockett). Each student reads different legends and any factual information they can find. Students share their information with their teammates, decide what is true and what is fiction, and create some way of sharing their character with the class (skit, a new legend, a puppet show, a radio play).

Corners

You can find **Corners** *in Lessons 1, 3, 4, 19*

Steps

1 Select a topic and name a few (usually four) alternatives associated with the topic. Assign each alternative to a different part of the classroom (usually the four corners).

2 Students select one of the alternatives and record it on a piece of paper.

3 Students go to the corners they choose. Students pair up and discuss their choice. Students can pair again for further discussion.

4 Students share and paraphrase across corner.

5 Students return to their teams and review the reasons each corner was selected.

Corners is a classbuilding structure which can be used in a wide variety of ways. It provides opportunities for students to learn something about the other students in their class and to begin to accept individual differences. With academic content, Corners can introduce a topic to the class, provide students an opportunity to discuss their opinion with others who agree with them, or provide an opportunity to summarize key points.

Corners is different than Similarity Groups, because in Corners the specific alternatives are given by the teacher and in Similarity Groups no specific alternatives are given.

Variations

Rather than have just one member from each corner paraphrase what was said in another corner, have each student paraphrase to a partner what was said.

Corners can be used as a team formation method. Students choose their response.

After students have shared and paraphrased, new groups are formed among the students in the same corner so that they can continue developing the ideas they share in common.

Hints

To prevent students from changing their minds and congregating with friends, be sure to have students write their choice on a piece of paper before leaving their seats.

Corners

Corners
A c t i v i t i e s

Prereading activity
Have students pick a choice of something associated with the story. For example, before reading *Ira Sleeps Over* by Bernard Waber ask the students what they would take with them if they were going to a friend's house.

Types of Books
Ask students what their favorite type of book is.

Mother Goose Characters
Ask students which Mother Goose character they associate most with.

Favorite Characters
Students choose the character in a book with whom they can most identify. For example from *Charlotte's Web*.

Story Setting
Students choose the setting for a story they are going to write.

Discussion Topics
What would you like to discuss more?

Predictions
Have three or four predictions about the next part of a book or story available for the students to choose from. Ask them to choose the corner that tells what they think will happen next in the story.

Jeanne Stone: *Cooperative Learning & Language Arts: A Multi-Structural Approach*
Kagan Publishing • 1 (800) 933-2667 • www.KaganOnline.com

31

Formations

You can find **Formations** *in Lesson 5*

Steps

1 The teacher announces and draws a shape or figure.

2 Students form the given shape or figure.

3 Students change the shape or figure as directed.

Formations has students form shapes or figures with their bodies by holding hands. Sometimes they are not allowed to talk. This can be done in teams or with the whole class. For primary classes, the teacher begins by marking the formation wanted on the ground and the students line up on the provided outline. As the students become more adept at creating the formations asked for, the teacher no longer needs to draw the outline for the students. As well as stationary figures, the teams or class can also make mobile figures. After forming an ice cream cone, the students show it melting. After creating a piano keyboard, the students pretend it is playing. After forming a kite, the students can show how it floats and flies in the breeze.

Formations
A c t i v i t i e s

Class Formations

Sentence Formation
With two or three teams working together, a sentence is dictated by the teacher. Some of the students hold individual word cards and others become the necessary punctuation marks. For example the sentence "The dog jumps." could be made by one team — three words and one punctuation mark. The sentence "Hi!" said Mary. "What are you doing tonight?" would take four teams of four (or fifteen people).

Story Problem
Form the scene that shows the problem the character encountered in the story.

Alphabet
Form a letter of the alphabet. What letter comes after _____? What letter comes before _____? What letter does _____ begin with?

Prereading
As a prewriting experience, the students can form something related to the theme. For example, make a bubble blowing tool, make your favorite food, make a formation that shows something great that could happen to you.

Punctuation
After the teacher reads a sentence, the students form the correct ending punctuation.

Spelling
Students "write out" a spelling word.

Team Formations

Character portrayal
Portray a character from the book.

Setting
Show the setting of the story.

Story Scene
In your team, decide on your favorite part of the story we just read. Using all four team members, make a scene (formation) so that the class can guess what part of the story it is.

Story Object
Create an object that best summarizes a character in the story you read. (Forming a porridge bowl for Goldilocks, a basket for Red Riding Hood, a glass slipper for Cinderella.)

Information Sharing
Among Teams

One Stray

*You can find **Information Sharing** in Lessons 8, 9, 16, 17, 21*

Teams Post

Each team sends a representative to the chalkboard or to a piece of chart paper to post their best answers simultaneously. The teams can continue working while some of their ideas are being recorded and shared with the class.

Carbon Sharing

When recording, students use sheets of carbon paper equal to the number of teams with which they will share. After the recording is complete, the students pass out the carbon copies to the other teams. This can be used equally well for team responses to be shared with other teams or individual responses to be shared with teammates.

One Stray

One Stray provides an opportunity for the students to share their ideas or product with the other teams. In each of the four rounds, one of the team members travels to another team to share his/her team's ideas or product with that team.

In Round 1, #1 travels with the team's ideas or product one team to the right (or left). #2, #3, and #4 stay and listen to the presentation by the visiting #1. All members return to the home teams.

In Round 2, #2 travels with the team's ideas or product two teams to the right (or left). #1, #3, and #4 stay and listen to the presentation by the visiting #2. All members return to the home teams.

In Round 3, #3 travels with the team's ideas or product three teams to the right (or left). #1, #2, and #4 stay and listen to the presentation by the visiting #3. All members return to the home teams.

In Round 4, #4 travels with the team's ideas or product four teams to the right (or left). #1, #2, and #3 stay and listen to the presentation by the visiting #4. All members return to the home teams.

Three Stray

One person from each team stays seated in the team's place while the other teams rotate from table to table. The team's representative shares the team's information with all the other teams as they rotate through.

Class Notebooks

Each team records their ideas on a three-ringed sheet of notebook paper. The sheet is placed in a three-ringed binder under a divider labeled with the topics being shared. The notebook is available for other teams to peruse.

Gallery Tour

Completed team products are displayed around the room. Near each product should be a sheet of paper for other groups to ask questions or write comments about the products. Each team stands in front of their own product in the classroom. At the teacher's signal, they pass from one product to the next until they have viewed all the products in the classroom. Students are encouraged to ask a question or make a comment about each product they see. Using small slips of paper, students make a record of the unique ideas they see on each product. Remind students that they don't need to list an idea twice. Students return to their team and discuss the common ideas they recorded from the products. They can also discuss any questions and comments the other students made about their product.

Roam-the-Room

At a given signal, all the students roam throughout the room, observing the products of the other teams. At a given signal, all students return to their teams and report on what they found in their roaming.

Stand-N-Share

Following a Group Discussion, each team makes sure that all their team members have an idea to share. All students in the class stand up. Starting on one side of the classroom, students begin sharing. As each person shares, he or she sits down. Anyone in the room who has the same idea or a similar idea sits down also. The sharing continues until all of the students are sitting down.

Share and Compare

Each team shares its best idea(s) with the team next to them.

Team Inside-Outside Circle

After forming inside and outside circles as teams (four teams on the inside, four teams on the outside, facing each other), the teams make their presentations to the team opposite them on the circle. After a response time for the first team, the other team presents and listens to the responses of the "audience." Before rotating to a new team for another presentation, the teams take a few minutes to work on improving their presentations.

Information Sharing

Jeanne Stone: *Cooperative Learning & Language Arts: A Multi-Structural Approach*
Kagan Publishing • 1 (800) 933-2667 • www.KaganOnline.com

37

Inside-Outside Circle

*You can find **Inside-Outside Circle** in Lessons 6, 7*

Steps

1 The students form two concentric circles.

2 The students face each other and discuss a topic, practice a skill, or share something about themselves.

3 The students rotate to the right or left and move around the circle to new partner.

Inside-Outside Circle has a variety of uses. It can be:

• A classbuilding activity to help the students in the class get acquainted. Some sample topics are: What is your name? What hobbies do you have? Where were you born? What television show do you like to watch? If you were going out to dinner tonight, where would you go?

• An activity to introduce a concept or have students share prior experience with a topic. Some sample topics are: Have you ever taken a trip? When do you use electricity at home? What would you expect to find on a farm?

• To share specific information about an activity or assignment about to be started or just completed. Some sample topics are: What do you think we might learn about ...? How did you feel during the lesson? Read your story to your partner and have him or her ask you a question about it. Tell what the hardest part of the assignment was for you? the easiest?

- To practice and learn. Listen to the sentence and tell your partner what the end punctuation should be. What punctuation is missing from this sentence (shown on overhead or chart)? Give two adjectives that describe Papa Bear. Change this sentence to the past tense, the future tense. Change this word by adding a prefix or a suffix and use the new word in a sentence.

For Inside-Outside Circle students stand in two concentric circles with the inside circle facing out and the outside circle facing in. Each student has a partner if there are an even number of students. For an uneven number of students, one pair on the outside circle become partners and together they rotate and share the same partner from the inside circle. The teacher provides a prompt. After completing the activity, the students make a quarter turn to the right (or left) and rotate to a new partner. Again the teacher provides the prompt and the process continues with the students rotating through different partners on the circle. The teacher can vary the rotation by changing the direction of the turn and the number of spaces passed on each rotation.

The prompts for Inside-Outside Circle can be presented in different ways. The teacher can ask a question or provide a topic for discussion after each rotation or the students can hold flashcards with the material to be learned. The students show their partners their flashcards and get a response before rotating. The flashcards can be traded after each turn to increase the number of practices the students receive.

Inside-Outside Circle

Inside-Outside Circle
A c t i v i t i e s

Introductory or Concept Development Actvities
Prior Experience
Share about a time you went hiking or for a walk. What did you see? Where did you go?

Favorite Color
What is your favorite color? Tell about how it makes you feel. What color makes you feel the opposite?

Favorite Animal
What is your favorite animal? Why?

Interests
Share what some things are that you like to do and you don't like to do.

Moving
Have you ever moved from one place to another? Why?

Practice Activities
Positive Language Experience
Show just the outside students something hidden in a box. With each rotation, the outside students give clues about what is in the box without telling what it is. After five or six turns, the inside circle guesses. Change roles. Show the inside students something and have them give clues to the outside students. To practice different parts of speech, the clues must be nouns, adjectives or verbs. If a sock was in the box, some noun clues might be foot, shoe, toes, slipper. Some verb clues might be walk, cover, pull on, stretch.

Vocabulary
Given a vocabulary word, have the students exchange synonyms or antonyms of the given word. Spell the word. Use the word in a sentence. This can be done with flashcards.

Punctuation
Show a flashcard with an end punctuation mark. The students must give a sentence that ends with that punctuation mark.

Preview/Review Activities
Story Review
Think about the story we just read (listened to). What character do you like? Where did the story take place? What might happen next? What character would you want to be in the story? What happened before this story?

Predicting
We will be reading the book *Harriet the Spy*. What do you think it might be about? If you had to classify it as a kind of book, how would you classify it? Have you ever said something about a friend and then changed your mind later?

Processing
How did you feel about participating in the last activity? What did the class do to make it a successful experience? What could the class have done to make it better?

Jigsaw

You can find **Jigsaw** *in Lessons 1, 12*

Jigsaw is a division of labor design with an emphasis on task specialization. Its main purpose is to have each team member become responsible for a specific piece of the learning, and then to share that piece with his or her teammates. Using Jigsaw focuses the student interaction during the lesson on interdependence, because each student only has access to one-fourth of the information needed to complete the lesson. Jigsaw can be used for a variety of purposes, including mastery, concept development, discussion and team projects.

There are many forms of Jigsaw and they can be used in a variety of ways, for a variety of goals. Each form of Jigsaw has specific steps that will lead to successful completion of the lesson. At each of these steps different cooperative learning structures can be used to guide the student interaction. Throughout this book, not all of the steps are used in each lesson.

The simplest form of Jigsaw is **Within-Team Jigsaw** with three steps.

Step 1
Each student from a team works independently to master a bit of new material.

Step 2
Students do a RoundRobin to share their knowledge with their teammates.

Step 3
There is an assessment of all students.

In Within-Team Jigsaw the students do not work with members of other teams. The students may need help in learning how to master material, to report the material to their teammates, and to tutor teammates for mastery.

Partner-Expert Group Jigsaw

Partner-Expert Group Jigsaw is similar to basic Jigsaw in that the curriculum material is divided into four parts and each team member is assigned one part. Beyond that, the students are given structured opportunities to compare notes with other students who are learning the same information. Partner-Expert Group Jigsaw follows these five steps:

Step 1
Each student is assigned a like-topic partner from another team.

Step 2
The partners meet to master the material.

Step 3
The partners pair to become an expert group to discuss the material, checking for completeness and agreement.

Step 4
The partners meet again to prepare and practice the presentation they will make to their teams.

Step 5
The teams meet and the members make their presentations.

Jigsaw

Jeanne Stone: *Cooperative Learning & Language Arts: A Multi-Structural Approach*
Kagan Publishing • 1 (800) 933-2667 • www.KaganOnline.com

Jigsaw
A c t i v i t i e s

Reading Within a Theme
Each team member can be responsible for reading a poem, story, or book on a given theme. After the independent reading is done, the team members can give a summary of the material they read and then discuss similarities and differences in the treatment of the theme and the conclusions they can draw from them.

Creating a Story Map
Assign each team member one of these elements from a story map. Each team member learns about an element, teaches it to his or her teammates and the team then creates a story map from a story they have read together.

Versions of a Story
Each team member can read a different version of the same story, and then the team can compare and contrast the stories, and discuss the conclusions that can be drawn from the information they have. For example, four versions of Cinderella can be used: *Cinderella* by Charles Perrault, *Cinderella* by Grimm, *Yeh-Shen* by Ai-ling Louie and "Tattercoats" in *More English Fairy Tales* edited by Joseph Jacobs.

Character Study
Each team member can become a specialist on one of the characters in the book (or story). The team can then create the "next" chapter, a different ending, or a dialogue that is true to the characters in the story, or they can retell the story from a different point of view.

Elements of Genre
When students are going to write using a specific mode of writing, each student learns a skill necessary for successfully completing that type of writing. For example, when preparing to write a tall tale, one student can learn about exaggeration, one about characterization, one about tall tales and their role in folklore, and one about the importance of realistic details.

Controversy Jigsaw
Using a story with four interpretations of an ending (for example, "The Lady and the Tiger"), all same-numbered team members meet to discuss a different interpretation. The team members return to their teams and discuss the different interpretations they have for the ending of the story.

Line-Ups

Steps

1 The teacher announces the topic and the poles of the Line-Up.

2 The students line up.

3 The students discuss their position in the line-up with a partner.

4 The students report to the class.

*You can find **Line-Ups** in Lessons 5, 14, 17*

Line-Ups can be used in a variety of ways: for classbuilding, to promote communication, to learn respect for individual differences, to develop concepts, and to create short-term teams. Basically, the teacher provides the prompt and sets the end dimensions. Students then line up in order of their responses. This order can relate to a characteristic (age, birthday, alphabetical, etc.), or to agreement (totally agree at one pole and totally disagree at the other). The whole class or individual teams may form a Line-up.

Characteristic Line-Ups are related to a specific measure of some kind. The characteristics used can vary a great deal. An example follows.

Time:	Line up by the number of minutes you read last night.
Number:	Line up by the number of books you read over summer vacation.
Alphabetical:	Line up alphabetically by the spelling word you are holding.
Measurement:	Line up by how tall you think the Jack's giant is.
Money:	Line up by how much money you think Alexander needs for a radio.

Often Characteristic Line-Ups are followed up with making a graph as a record of the students' responses.

Variations
Value Line-Ups

Value Line-Ups or Agree-Disagree Line-Ups, allow students to respond as to how much they agree or disagree with a given statement. After the teacher makes a statement and sets the end dimensions (agree on one side of the room and disagree on the other), the students line up by how much they agree or disagree with the given statement. The statements can be teacher-created or can be a character's statements taken from the piece of literature being studied. For example:

from *The Hatchet* by Gary Paulsen:
"I'm hungry and I'd trade every thing I have for a hamburger."

from *The Empty Pot* by Demi:
"You did your best, and your best is good enough to present to the Emperor."

a teacher's statement:
"Goldilocks should be prosecuted for breaking and entering."
"My friends are the same as I am."

Before lining up students can mark their position on a Value Line at their desk.

Extensions
To encourage more student interaction, Line-Ups can be folded or split to expose students to ideas different than their own.

Folded Value Lines
After students have shared with someone near them in line, the student on one end of the line begins walking toward the opposite end of the line to pair up the student on the far end. The students follow the leader until the line stops and they are each facing a new partner. Folded Value Lines offer those with opposing views an opportunity to interact with each other. Those in the middle (who have the same view) can predict and discuss what the opposing students may be discussing.

Split Value Line
After students have shared with someone near them in line, the line splits in the middle. A middle student walks back along the line with the other students following. Students stop and face a new partner. Split Value Lines allow those students who can see an issue two ways or who have no strong opinion to interact with those students who have a very strong opinion.

Line-ups

Line-Ups
A c t i v i t i e s

Names
Line up in alphabetical order by first name or last name.

Spelling Words
Pass out spelling word cards. Line up alphabetically by word cards.

Prereading or Prewriting Experience
Line up by the number of times you _____. This can be a prereading or prewriting experience. It gives a great picture of how much background information the class has. Some examples might be: how often have you ridden a horse, spent the night at a friend's house (before reading *Ira Sleeps Over* by Bernard Waber), or been stranded (*Island of the Blue Dolphins* by Scott O'Dell).

Favorite Author
Line up alphabetically by the author of your favorite book.

Books
Line up by the number of books you read over vacation.

Opinions
If you were Jack from *Jack and the Beanstalk* how many times would you have climbed the beanstalk and gone to the giant's castle?

Sentence Length
Given a theme, students write a sentence about the theme. Encourage them to write as long a sentence as possible. Have the students line up by the length of their sentences. They can share their sentence with a partner standing next to them or the line can be folded so that those with the shortest sentences can interact with those with the longest sentences. This can lead into a discussion of sentence expansion and/or sentence combining.

Sound Volume
Have students think of sounds associated with the story they have read or with a holiday (this works especially well at Halloween). Have them line up by the volume of the sound — loud to soft.

Fact or Opinion
After reading an article students line up by how much they think the article is fact (one pole) or opinion (another pole).

Author Review
After reading a number of books by the same author, rate the author on a scale of one to ten on how well you like his or her books. Be prepared to tell why and give examples.

Computers
Do you agree or disagree with teaching students how to use computers for word processing?

Key Statements
Do you agree or disagree with this statement from *The Diary of Anne Frank* by Anne Frank, "In spite of everything, I still believe that people are really good at heart." (A key statement from any core literature work may be substituted.)

Mix-Freeze-Group

Steps

1 The students <u>mix</u> in the center of the room.

2 The teacher calls "<u>Freeze</u>" and announces the group size.

3 The students form <u>groups</u>.

4 (Optional) The students discuss a topic provided by the teacher.

Mix-Freeze-Group is a classbuilding and mastery structure. It provides an opportunity for students to move about the classroom meeting other students and engaging in a discussion with the students in their group. The teacher asks the students to "Mix" (mingle) in an open area of the classroom. On the "Freeze" signal, the students stop where they are, and then "Group" by the number (or problem) the teacher gives. For example, "Mix .... Freeze .... How many blind mice are there?" Students form groups of three. "Mix .... Freeze .... What is (two claps) times (three claps)?" Students form groups of six. "Mix .... Freeze .... Group by fours." Students form groups of four.

Jeanne Stone: *Cooperative Learning & Language Arts: A Multi-Structural Approach*
Kagan Publishing • 1 (800) 933-2667 • www.KaganOnline.com

51

When the groups are formed, there are times when the students do not evenly divide into the given group size. In those instances, set a "Lost and Found" area near where the teacher is standing. Any student that does not fit evenly into a group, stands in the Lost and Found area. As the students regroup the next time, any student in the Lost and Found must be incorporated into one of the new groups. The rule is that the same student cannot be in the Lost and Found two times in a row.

When using Mix-Freeze-Group as a class-building activity, once students are in their groups, they can simply go around the group saying their names and sharing something about themselves (favorite color, favorite television show, number of brothers and sisters, etc). As a mastery activity, once students are in their groups they would practice whatever the skill was by answering the question given by the teacher, showing flashcards to each other, or asking each other questions.

Variation
Mix-Freeze-Pair

Mix-Freeze-Pair is a set variation of Mix-Freeze-Group. The group size is set and every time the students regroup, they group into pairs. This has several advantages. For team formation, after a number of mixes, the pairs can pair and form a random team of four. When using flashcards (with spelling words, parts of speech, sentences to punctuate, vocabulary words to practice), the students exchange flashcards each turn, thus providing varying practice.

Mix-freeze-group

Mix-Freeze-Group
A c t i v i t i e s

Names
Share what you like about your name.

Rainbow Rounds
Each time the students freeze, name a color. They group by the number of letters in the color word and share things that are that color. For example: The teacher says "blue," the students group by four and name things that are blue.

How Many?
The teacher prompts the group size and the response with statements such as "Name three chores you have to do at home." "Name five presents you would like to get for your birthday." "Name four ways to make a sandwich without bread." "Name two words to describe _____ (a character in a book or story that has been read)."

When I Grow Up
Each student shares what they would like to be when they grow up and why. This can include a discussion of the education they would need, the skills they would have to have, and the subjects in school they would use the most.

Sounds Abound
Students fold a paper into four sections and write the name of an object in each section. Each time they group, they discuss the different sounds the object would make and record them on their paper. When the paper is complete, they use the sounds to write a story complete with sound effects.

The Answer Is "No!"
Students share questions that have a "No" answer.

Facts and Opinions
On a topic given by the teacher, the students share a fact or an opinion.

A Friend Is...
Students share attributes a friend has.

Headline Alert
Have each student find a picture in a newspaper or magazine. Each time they group, students create different headlines for the pictures they see.

Riddles
Students write "Guess Who?" riddles about the topic being studied (a book, a story, an animal, a classmate for classbuilding). Each time they pair, they share their riddle and their partner has three guesses to guess the riddle.

Numbered Heads Together

*You can find **Numbered Heads** in Lessons 2, 6, 10, 13, 14, 15, 16, 21*

Steps

1 The students number off.

2 The teacher poses the question.

3 The students put their heads together and discuss the answer.

4 The teacher calls a number.

Numbered Heads Together is a simple four-step structure. Its main strength is in building mastery and in reviewing previously learned information. In step one, the students number off from one to four. On a team of only three, team member #3 answers when numbers three and four are called. On a team of five, team members #4 and #5 both answer when number four is called. The teacher then asks a high consensus question. Rather than asking a simple knowledge or comprehension question (Who is the main character in *Stone Fox*?), ask a question with multiple responses (Make sure everyone on your team can name at least one reason why Bobby ran away). In step three, the students put their heads together, discuss the correct answer, and make sure that everyone knows the answer. In step four, the teacher calls a number and those students raise their hands to respond.

Variations

These are a variety of response models that can be alternatively used with Numbered Heads Together.

Thumbs Up

After a student responds, the teacher can have the others agree or disagree with a thumbs up or thumbs down.

Shared Responses

In a multiple-part answer, the teacher can have students from different groups each give part of the response.

Simultaneous Response

All the students can simultaneously give the answer on the count of three.

Blackboard Response

All students responding can write the answers on the chalkboard or on a group slate.

Adding On

After an incomplete response, the teacher can ask for another person to add to the answer.

Hints

When a teacher asks a question and only a couple of the teams respond, the teacher should have all the teams put their heads back together. The teacher might say "Not enough #2's have their hands up, put your heads together and make sure all #2's can answer the question."

Vary the order of numbers called to respond by using a spinner, dice or pulling numbers from a hat.

Numbered Heads

Jeanne Stone: *Cooperative Learning & Language Arts: A Multi-Structural Approach*
Kagan Publishing • 1 (800) 933-2667 • www.KaganOnline.com

Numbered Heads
A c t i v i t i e s

Parts of Speech
Be able to name three good verbs (adjectives) to use with _____ (a particular character in a story or book).

Overused Words
Be sure everyone can name a word that can substitute for run, said, good, etc.

Parts of Speech
When reviewing or practicing parts of speech, use three rounds to build progressively harder questions. First round, decide if an underlined word in a sentence is a particular part of speech. For example, "The dog is brown. Is brown an adjective?" Second round, students name the particular part of speech in the sentence. For example, "Carrie always forgets to tie her shoes. Which word is the adverb?" Third round, students name a particular part of speech. For example, "Make sure everyone in your group can name a noun."

Irregular Verbs or Plural Nouns
Students can review irregular verbs or plural nouns.

Homonyms
Use homonyms in sentences. "Make sure everyone in your group can give a sentence for *new* and *knew*."

Story Review
After reading a story, review the parts of the plot. For example, make sure everyone on your team can name the character(s), the climax, the problem, the setting, the theme

Vocabulary Review
For vocabulary review, students can give the synonym or antonym of a word. They can use it in a sentence. They can spell it. They can add the missing work in a sentence. They can replace a given word in a sentence.

Punctuation Review
Students can review various punctuation marks in context of writing. Place an excerpt from student writing on an overhead or on a chart. Ask questions regarding punctuating the text. Where do the periods go? Where should the quotation marks go? Where should the comma go?

Capital Letters
Students can tell where to add capital letters in a given sentence.

Skill Review
Before beginning a writing session, review the types of punctuation or capital letters that may be needed. For example, "Make sure everyone in your group can name a place you will need to use a comma when you write your letter." "What things will you need to capitalize in your letter?"

Partners

You can find **Partners** *in Lessons 13, 19*

Steps

1 Partners are formed within teams.

2 The class divides so that same-topic partners are sitting on the same side of the classroom.

3 The materials are distributed.

4 The students master the material.

5 The partners consult with other same-topic partners.

6 The partners prepare to present and tutor the material they learned.

7 The teams reunite. Each set of partners shares their materials and tutors their teammates.

8 Team processing

9 Individual assessment

10 Improvement scoring and recognition.

Partners is a division of labor design with an emphasis on learning together and sharing the material learned with teammates. During Partners, two members on each team work together to learn one half of the material, while the other two members work together to learn the other half of the material. The partners return to their teams and teach each other. While the partners are learning the materials, same-topic partners from all the teams sit on the same side of the room, so that they can consult with other same-topic partners.

 Teacher's Note: In this book only the first seven steps of Partners are incorporated into the lessons.

Partners
A c t i v i t i e s

Author or Illustrator Study
Each set of partners can study books or stories written (or illustrated) by the same author. After sharing the content (or illustrations) with their teammates, they can discuss the similarities in the stories (or illustrations).

Writing Mechanics
Each set of partners can learn a different mechanics skill (commas, capital letters, periods, apostrophes) that will be needed in the writing lesson. They can return to their teams and teach the skill to their teammates.

Comparing Versions of a Story
Each set of partners can read a different version of something. When they return to their teams, they teach each other the story or information they have learned and compare it. For example, one set of partners can read *The Gingerbread Boy* and one can read *Journey Cake, Ho!* by Ruth Sawyer. In the upper grades, one set of partners can read sections of *Zia* by Scott O'Dell and the other can read factual information about Indian life at the early California missions.

Brainstorming with the Senses
After describing the topic, the teacher assigns different senses to each set of partners. Working with same-topic partners, the students brainstorm as many images as they can that deal with the sense and topic they have. For example, if the topic was "Fall," the teacher could assign one set of partners Hear, Smell and Feel and the other set of partners Taste and See. Students list as many images, objects, feelings, etc. as they can pertaining to Fall and each sense. When the teams reunite, they share the lists and describe Fall to a person visiting from another planet.

Poetry
Each set of partners can read and discuss a poem on a given topic. The partners can reunite, share their poems and discuss the different authors' interpretations of the same theme.

Jeanne Stone: *Cooperative Learning & Language Arts: A Multi-Structural Approach*
Kagan Publishing • 1 (800) 933-2667 • www.KaganOnline.com

61

RoundRobin

You can find **RoundRobin** *in Lessons 1, 2, 6, 7, 8, 9, 10, 11, 12, 13, 15, 17, 18, 20, 21, 22*

Steps

1 The teacher poses a problem.

2 The students, each in turn, orally share a response.

RoundRobin is a simple, yet effective, two-step cooperative learning structure. It is directly related to RoundTable — RoundRobin uses oral responses and RoundTable uses written responses. In step one, the teacher asks a question with many possible answers and in step two, the students orally respond in turn to share possible answers for the question. Team members can help the student who is responding if he or she requests help. RoundRobin can also be used for sharing information. For example, "Share something about your Grandma."

Roundrobin can be used frequently during a lesson format. It can be used to set the focus for the lesson, facilitate guided and independent practice, and help check for understanding.

Variations

Rallyrobin or Paired RoundRobin use partners on each team to alternate responses. For example, to practice telling a story, the partners would be looking at the same picture book and would alternate telling about each page of the story.

RoundRobin
A c t i v i t i e s

Prewriting Activity
Share ideas about an activity, event, field trip, etc. This can be part of prewriting.

Descriptive Words
Share descriptive words on a topic.

Story Review
After reading a story, comment on _____.

Color Words
Share objects that are a given color.

Storytelling
RoundRobin retelling a story just heard.

All About Me
Tell something about yourself — favorite color, sport, hobby.

Today I'm Wearing…
Each person describes one of their articles of clothing during each round.

Rhyming Words
List words that rhyme with (fall, can, hit, etc.)

How to…
Give the steps for a simple activity. For example, how to carve a jack-o-lantern, how to decorate a Christmas tree, how to make a peanut butter and jelly sandwich, etc.

Initial Consonant Sounds
As a basket or tub is passed around the table, each student selects an item or picture and tells its initial consonant (or vowel) sound.

Stories in the Round
Each person adds a sentence to a story, trying to keep it going as long as possible.

RoundTable

You can find RoundTable in Lessons 6, 7, 9, 16, 19

Steps

1 The teacher poses a problem.

2 The students, each in turn, write a response.

RoundTable is the written counterpart of RoundRobin. In step one, the teacher asks a question with many possible answers and in step two, the students respond in turn to make a list of possible answers for the question. During RoundTable, students pass a single sheet of paper and a single pencil around the table to record responses. Team members may assist the one who is responding if help is requested.

RoundTable, like RoundRobin, may be used frequently throughout a lesson. It is great as an anticipatory set, and may be used to facilitate guided and independent practice, and help check for understanding.

Variations

Sequential RoundTable is done with one paper and one pencil.

Simultaneous RoundTable is done with two, three, or four papers and pencils.

RoundTable activity is used to complete a group activity or project that requires putting together pieces in order. For example: Each student in turn adds to a picture that is showing the setting for a story. — or— Each student in turn chooses a word from his or her word bank to pass on the page to increase the length of the sentence.

RallyTable is done with partners on each team passing a paper back and forth for responses. For example, if you were going to compare and contrast raisins and marshmallows, one set of partners might be rallytabling words that describe marshmallows and the other set of partners words that describe raisins.

Hints

- Be certain the question is open ended enough that there will be many responses.

- Be certain students understand the type of response you are asking for.

- When checking for understanding, include some way of monitoring the students' responses. For example: Teams can trade papers for a Team Review after the RoundTable is completed. Use Numbered Heads Together briefly to review responses from the RoundTable list.

RoundTable

RoundTable
A c t i v i t i e s

Prewriting Idea Cache
List facts about an activity, event, field trip, etc. This can be part of prewriting.

Descriptive Words
List or tell descriptive words on a topic.

Overused Words
List words that can be used to replace an overused word such as run, said, or good.

Comparisons
List comparisons: round as _____; as white as _____.

Listing Words in Categories
List words in a given category: jobs, flowers, foods, etc.

Main Ideas and Details
With a given idea from a story or experience, students add supporting details.

Parts of Speech
List a specific usage function: nouns, verbs, adjectives, statements, exclamations, proper nouns, verbs and past tense forms, etc., and students roundTable words that fit that part of speech.

Picture Prompt
List ideas about a picture prompt.

Ideas for a News Article
Use a story part at the top of each page: Who? What? When? Where? Why? How?

Opening Lines
Each student creates an opening line for a story. The students do Simultaneous RoundTable as each student is simultaneously adding a new sentence to each story.

Step-by-Step
Students write step-by-step ideas for an activity.

Jeanne Stone: *Cooperative Learning & Language Arts: A Multi-Structural Approach*
Kagan Publishing • 1 (800) 933-2667 • www.KaganOnline.com

67

Similarity Groups

*You can find **Similarity Groups** in Lessons 2, 4, 5, 10, 13, 20*

Steps

1 The teacher announces the dimension.

2 The students think of their specific response.

3 The students group with others who have the same response.

Similarity Groups involves students with each other and gives them a chance to create their own preference. To begin Similarity Groups, the teacher announces a dimension such as color hair, birthday month or favorite T.V. show. Everyone with the same characteristic or preference forms a group. The students in each group pair up and discuss the positive and negative aspects of the characteristic. It can include paraphrasing across groups. Similarity Groups can be followed by frequency graphs to provide a good visual description of the class.

Similarity Groups is different than Corners in that there are no set characteristics given to provide the basis of forming groups. There could be two groups, or there could be ten groups.

Hint

Have students write their responses on small sheets of paper before leaving their seats. It prevents students from "changing" their minds and grouping with friends.

Similarity Groups
A c t i v i t i e s

Favorite Tales
Their favorite fairy tales, myths, legends, or tall tales.

The "Next" Chapter
Ideas they have for a "next" chapter in a book. The chapter that comes after the book is finished.

Prior Experiences
Experiences they have had related to the theme.

Predictions
Their predictions as to what a book or story will be about after seeing only the cover and the title.

Favorite Character
Their favorite character in a story or book. These groups can then be used to begin a study of character analysis.

Favorite Part of the Book
Their favorite part of a book (story).

Predictions
Their predictions as to what will happen next in the book (story) they are reading.

Character's Reasons
Reasons they feel the character has for doing what he or she does.

Genre
The type of genre they wish to read in exploring the theme (non-fiction, short story, poetry, novel) the class will study.

Sorting

You can find **Sorting** *in Lesson 18*

Steps

1 The students brainstorm ideas on separate pieces of paper.

2 The students sort the ideas.

3 The students share their category systems.

Sorting allows the students to organize information in a variety of forms and methods. Creating a variety of sorting systems allows students to stretch their cognitive skills. As students use sorting in different situations and with different topics, they begin to see common category systems, such as Venn diagrams, 2x2 matrix, tree diagram, and plot. After sorting, the ideas the students developed are readily available for a reading or writing task.

To begin, students brainstorm and record ideas on small pieces of paper — one idea per piece. The ideas can be generated in many different ways: Brainstorming, Roundtable, Word Webbing, etc. Encourage students to list as many ideas as possible. After they have several dozen ideas, stop the students.

Jeanne Stone: *Cooperative Learning & Language Arts: A Multi-Structural Approach*
Kagan Publishing • 1 (800) 933-2667 • www.KaganOnline.com

71

Students place the ideas in the center of the team so that everyone on the team can see. Students sort the ideas, checking for consensus, before placing an idea in a category. When finished, each category is labeled. The students can be limited to a specific number of categories (Sort your ideas into three categories) or to specific categories (Sort your ideas by size).

The students tour the room, looking at the different ways the other teams sorted their ideas. The students return to their teams and resort their ideas using different categories (maybe ones they had seen used by another team). This can be repeated several times.

Variations

Unstructured Sorts: The students are not given any criteria for their sorting. The content for Unstructured Sorts can be anything: ideas about a story, vocabulary or spelling words, books, etc.

Structured Sorts: Structured Sorts provides the category system the students will use to sort their ideas. Some common category systems are Venn diagrams, Tree Diagrams, Unipolar Category, etc. To help guide the learning, students may even be given specific categories to use when sorting.

Ways to Share Category Systems

Teams Share: Each team shares its categories with the team next to them.

Gallery Tour: The completed categories are displayed on each team's desks. Near each category system is a sheet of paper for other groups to ask questions or write comments about the categories. Each team stands in front of their own desks. At the teacher's signal, they pass from one category system to the next until they have viewed all the category systems. Students are encouraged to ask a question or make a comment about each category system they see. Using small slips of paper, students make a record of the categories they see. Remind students that they don't need to list a category twice. Students return to their team and discuss the categories they recorded. They can also discuss any questions and comments the other students made about their sorting.

Three Stay: Three Stay provides an opportunity for the students to share their categories with the other teams. In each of the four rounds, one of the team members travels to another team to share his or her team's categories with that team. In Round One, #1 travels with the team's categories one team to the right (or left). #2, #3, and #4 stay and listen to the categories as shared by the visiting #1. All members return to the home teams. In Round Two, #2 travels with the team's categories two teams to the right (or left). #1, #3, and #4 stay and listen to the categories as shared by the visiting #2. All members return to the home teams. In Round Three, #3 travels with the team's categories three teams to the right (or left). #1, #2, and #4 stay and listen to the categories as shared by the visiting #3. All members return to the home teams. In Round Four, #4 travels with the team's categories four teams to the right (or left). #1, #2, and #3 stay and listen to the categories as shared by the visiting #4. All members return to the home teams.

Sorting

Jeanne Stone: _Cooperative Learning & Language Arts: A Multi-Structural Approach_
Kagan Publishing • 1 (800) 933-2667 • www.KaganOnline.com

One Stay: One person from each team stays seated in each team's place while the other team members rotate through the room. The team's representative shares the team's categories with the visiting teams.

Roam-the-Room: At a given signal, all the students move throughout the room observing the category systems of the other teams. At a given signal, all students return to their teams and report on what they have found in their roaming.

Sorting

Jeanne Stone: *Cooperative Learning & Language Arts: A Multi-Structural Approach*
Kagan Publishing • 1 (800) 933-2667 • www.KaganOnline.com

73

Sorting
A c t i v i t i e s

Organize Information
Given set categories, students can organize information before writing.

Character Study
Students can brainstorm about the different characters in the story (or stories), each character on a different color paper. All the descriptors can then be sorted to find similarities and differences among the characters.

Parts of Speech
After brainstorming words about a topic, they can be sorted by parts of speech to create an easy to use word bank.

Compare and Contrast
After reading a group of stories on the same theme, students can brainstorm ideas associated with the stories to find similarities and differences among the stories.

Story Elements
Students can sort things associated with a story and have it lead to the main elements of a story — characters, setting, problem, and solution.

Presenting Information
Students can sort information to find the best way of presenting it — compare, contrast, report of information or evaluation.

Team Discussion

You can find **Team Discussion** *in Lessons* ***2, 3, 5, 6, 7, 8, 10, 12, 14, 15, 16, 17, 18, 20, 22***

Steps

1 The teacher presents a low-consensus topic.

2 Students discuss the topic within their teams.

3 Teams share their conclusions with another team or with the class.

Team Discussion is a two-step structure for discussing an issue or question presented by the teacher. In step one, the teacher asks a low-consensus question and in step two, the students talk it over. Following the Team Discussion, students share their ideas with the class. The key issue is to share with as much student interaction as possible.

Variations

Simultaneous Share: One member of each team records a response on the chalkboard or on a chart paper when their team is finished.

Team Notebooks: The teams record their ideas in a team notebook to be looked at later by the teacher and/or other teams.

Teams Share: Each team shares with the team next to it.

Stand-Up and Share: All students discuss an issue until all members of the team have an idea to share. Everyone stands up. Quickly the students begin to share around the classroom. After a student shares, he or she sits down as well as anyone else in the class that had the same idea or one similar to it.

Lightbulb!: The teacher asks students who feel that they have something insightful or important to share.

For other methods of sharing, see ***Simultaneous Share.***

Team Discussion
A c t i v i t i e s

Alternate Settings
Discuss what would happen if the author changed the setting? Could the story still possibly happen in another setting?

Prediction
What do you think this story will be about?

Giving an Opinion
In the twenty-first century, books become a scarce commodity, how will that change our lives?

Connections
We have just finished reading a number of books, discuss why these books were linked in the same unit. What similarites and/or differences were there?

Letter to the Principal
Discuss what improvements you would like to see made at school. Which of these might you be able to include in a letter to the principal?

Theme
What do you think the author's theme is in this book?

Sequel
If there was a sequel to this book, what do you think it would be about?

Opinion
Listen to this story, what do you think about _____?

Character Prediciton
If you were (a character), what would you do in this situation?

Sequence of Events
How would this story have been different if the sequence of events had been altered? For example, what might have happened if Charlotte wrote her last word before Wilbur went to the fair?

Imagine that . . .
Imagine you are a _____. Discuss what life would be like.

Team Interview

You can find **Team Interview** *in Lessons 4, 12, 23*

Steps

1 One student is interviewed by his or her teammates.

2 In turn around the team, each student is interviewed.

Team Interview is similar to Roundrobin and Three-Step Interview. The students share around the team as in Roundrobin, while each student is given an allotted time and the teammates ask questions as in Three-Step Interview. For Team Interview, one team member stands in the center of the team (or sits in a designated seat). That person is interviewed by the other teammates. After the allotted time, the teacher signals, the students rotate, and a different team member is interviewed. Team Interview continues until all the team members have been interviewed. When a team has fewer members than the other teams in the class, the final round(s) can be used to go back to ask additional questions or to ask for clarification of responses.

Jeanne Stone: *Cooperative Learning & Language Arts: A Multi-Structural Approach*
Kagan Publishing • 1 (800) 933-2667 • www.KaganOnline.com

79

Team Interview
A c t i v i t i e s

Sharing Favorites
Each student is interviewed about their favorite color, sport, vacation spot, book, character, setting, etc.

Personal Experiences
Students can interview each other to find out what background experiences they have that relate to the topic being studied. This can happen just one time or in a series of interviews. For example, in studying about moving and the change in creates: If you could move anywhere you wanted, where would you move? Have you ever moved? What feelings did you have about moving? What were the best and the worst parts of moving?

Common Experiences
Each student shares an experience similar to one that was read about.

Role Play
Students each take the role of a character in a book or story they have read. They are interviewed in role. The interviewers are usually not in role.

Guess Who?
Each student is interviewed in role, but does not say what the role is. The teammates ask questions to guess who the student is. The number of questions can be limited as well as the time allotted for the interview.

Parts of Speech
Each student chooses or is assigned a part of speech. The team members ask questions about usage, and ask for examples of the part of speech.

Vocabulary Quiz
Each student draws a vocabulary word. The other team members ask questions to figure out what the word is.

Looking for the Main Idea
Each student chooses a main idea from an envelope. At the beginning of the interview, the student shares one detail that supports the main idea. Through questioning and other examples of supporting details, the other team members guess the main idea.

Developing Ideas During Prewriting
Each student shares the topic they want to write about. The other team members ask questions about the topic.

Famous Characters
Each team member receives a strip with the name of a famous character or person (Mother Goose, Batman, Luke Skywalker, President Clinton). The student is interviewed about that character. After all the interviews are complete, the team mixes the cards and passes them out again. Each team member shares what they heard about the character whose strip they now hold.

Team Project

You can find **Team Project** *in Lessons 4, 5, 13, 16, 19*

Team Project is very useful for the completion of a simple project. Team projects should be short and easy. Students should be able to complete the project anywhere from a few minutes to a class period. Roles may be given to each member of the team to ensure equal participation and individual accountability during the project. For example, each student may be required to use a different color marker on the project and all of the colors must be used equally. When a variety of materials will be used on the project, assign each team member a responsibility for one of the materials. Social roles can also be assigned separately or in tandem with material roles. Some sample roles are:

Material-Related Roles
#1 Scissors
#2 Paper
#3 Glue or paste, staples, tape, etc.
#4 Markers, crayons, pencils, etc.

Social Roles
#1 Taskmaster
#2 Praiser
#3 Materials Monitor
#4 Recorder

Students need to know, at the outset, that each team member must have a role in the presentation of the project to the class. Presentations can take many forms such as Gallery Tour, Teams Review, Team Inside-Outside Circle, and One Stray.

Note: If the project involves more than one class period or more complex structuring of individual team members' tasks, it is recommended that the teacher use the steps of Co-op Co-op, rather than use Team Project.

Team Project

Team Project
A c t i v i t i e s

Rainy Day Activity
Design a Rainy Day Activity Kit for someone who is their age (or younger or older). The kit must include a list of materials and any instructions for use.

Create a Monster
Create a monster that could live "where the wild things are" (*Where the Wild Things Are* by Maurice Sendak).

Space Explorers
Students design a rocket ship that could take them to unexplored areas of the galaxies. Each team member has a special job on the rocket ship. From the point of view required by their particular job, each team member writes a log about the trip taken on the rocket.

Favorite Scene
The teams discuss and agree on their favorite scene from a book or story. They then create a mural of this scene.

Word Ladders
Each team selects an idea based on the theme or topic being studied in the classroom. The team then selects a magazine picture that exemplifies the topic and creates a word ladder that can be used by the whole class. For example:

Sequence
Using given illustrations (or the students can create their own), students sequence the events that occur in a story.

Circle Stories
Some stories such as *If You Give a Mouse a Cookie* by Laura Joffe Numeroff are called circle stories, because they begin and end in the same place. Have the students diagram one of these stories using a large circle.

Book Poster
In *Homer Price* by Robert McCloskey, Homer is overloaded with doughnuts in his uncle's diner. Design a poster that could be used to sell the doughnuts. Each team member chooses one color to use and all colors must appear on the finished poster.

A List of Reasons
Make a list of all the reasons you can think of for not growing up (*Peter Pan* by J. M. Barrie).

Noise Factory
Each student brings two or three objects that make some kind of noise from home. The team sequences the objects in some way and records them on a tape. The team then writes a story using the sounds in the order they appear on the tape. Rather than writing a story, the team can prepare a skit using the actual sounds.

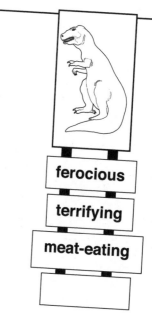

Team Word-Webbing

You can find **Team Word-Webbing** in Lessons **4, 5, 10**

Steps

1 Write the topic in the center of the paper.

2 RoundRobin to create core concepts around the topic.

3 Free-for-all to complete the word-web.

Team Word-Webbing (or Clustering or Semantic Mapping) is a powerful tool in concept development and information exchange. Each team has a large sheet of butcher paper or chart paper. Each student has a different color pen. The main topic is written in the center of the paper in a rectangle. The team members RoundTable once to add core concepts in ovals around the main topic. Then the team has a free-for-all adding details and making bridges between ideas.

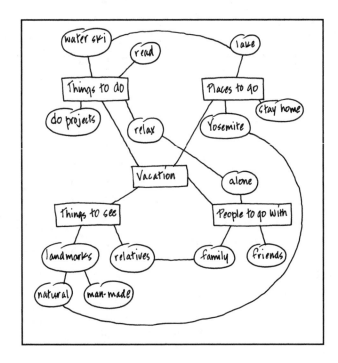

Team Word-Webbing
A c t i v i t i e s

Story Elements
Students can word-web the elements of a story.

Prewriting
Students can word-web a topic after a hands-on prewriting experience.

Exploring Theme
After reading several writings (books, poems, plays, stories) on a theme, students can word-web to begin exploring the connections between the writings and the theme.

Organizing Ideas
After Brainstorming and Categorizing, students can word-web to create their own organization of the ideas.

Character Study
Students use a character as a main topic. The core concepts are qualities the character has. During the free-for-all, the students add examples, other qualities, relationships between other characters, etc.

Overused Words
Start with an overused word in the center (said, run, nice, good), add a variety of emotions and word-web other ways to express the mood through a different word. For example, when working with "said," yelled would connect to anger, whispered would connect to fright, laughed would connect with happy.

Investigating a Book
Students use a word-web to organize ideas about the different elements in a book.

Holiday Madness
Students word-web ideas associated with a holiday by using the holiday as the topic and the senses (See, Touch, Hear, Smell, Taste) as the core concepts. The resulting word-web can be used for follow-up reading and writing activities.

Think-Pair-Share

You can find **Think-Pair-Share** *in Lessons 2, 6, 9, 12, 13, 16, 18, 20, 23*

Steps

1 The teacher poses a problem or asks a question.

2 Students think about the answer.

3 Students pair up and discuss their responses.

4 Students share their answers with the class.

Think-Pair-Share offers all students an opportunity to express their response to a question or discussion topic. In a traditional classroom, the teacher asks a question and only one or two students have the opportunity to respond. Using Think-Pair-Share, the teacher asks a question and gives the students think time. (The length of the think time varies as to the complexity of the question or problem.) At the teacher's signal, the students share their answers with partners, allowing all students to respond. Students are then invited to share their responses with the whole class.

The flexibility and power of Think-Pair-Share makes it easy to implement and use in the classroom. Students can be seated anywhere in the classroom: at a class meeting, in desks, in their teams, in line, etc. Every time the teacher stops to ask a question or invite a response, the students are actively involved with the lesson. To encourage individual accountability, the teacher can vary the way the responses are shared with in the classroom.

Methods for Sharing with the Whole Class

- *Think-Pair-Square*
  After students finish their discussion with a partner, two pairs meet (or square) to share.

- Write responses on chart paper.

- Do a quick whip through the class. (Students respond quickly one right after another.)

- *Stand-N-Share*
  All students stand up. As each student gives his or her response, he or she sits down. Anyone with a similar response sits down also. Continue until everyone is seated.

- Turn and share with a student in another group.

- Lightbulb! The teacher asks students who feel that they have something insightful or important to share.

Think-Pair-Share

Think-Pair-Share
A c t i v i t i e s

Sharing a Writing Topic
Students can share an idea for a story they want to write. After input from a variety of prewriting activities, students begin to formulate some of their ideas and share them with a partner.

Literature Discussion
Before, during or after reading a literature selection, students can respond to a variety of questions:
- What do you think will happen next?
- If you were (one of the characters), what would you do next? How would you feel?
- What do you think the story will be about?
- What other way could this story have ended?

Sentence Combining
When doing sentence combining activities, students can think about how they would combine the sentences and then share their thoughts with a partner.

Dear _____
Students pick their favorite character in a book or story. Have students think about what they would say in a letter to the character.

Topic Share
Students think about their writing topic. After sharing it with a friend, there is another think time in which the students think of questions they would ask about their partner's writing topic. The partners ask each other their questions. It actually becomes Think-Pair-Think-Pair-Share.

What If...?
Pose "What If...?" questions to the students. These can relate to a theme being discussed in the language arts class, topics to be used for classbuilding or teambuilding, or classroom problems that can arise. For example:
- What if you had one thousand dollars to spend?
- What if you won the lottery?
- What if you could pick any animal for a pet?
- What if you found a magic lamp and rubbed it?
- What if you were missing something from your desk?

Vocabulary Review
Announce a word and have the students think of a sentence, the definition, a synonym, an antonym, the spelling, etc.

Relating to a Character
Ask the students to think about how they are similar to one of the characters in the story. Students share the character they are similar to and why they think that way.

What Are They Saying?
Show the students a picture and have them think about what the characters would be saying to each other.

Draw What's Next
Stop at turning points in a story. Instead of having the students share what might happen next, have them draw what they think will happen next and then describe their picture to a partner. This actually becomes Think-Draw-Pair-Share.

Three-Step Interview

Steps

1 In pairs, one student interviews the other.

The students reverse roles.

3 In their teams of four, the students RoundRobin to share what they learned from their partner.

You can find **Three-Step Interview** *in Lessons 2, 4, 5, 11, 13, 14, 15, 17, 19, 20, 21, 22, 23*

Three-Step Interview is a simple information sharing structure. It works best in groups of four, but can be easily adapted to groups of three or groups of five. In Step 1, the students are in pairs; one is the interviewer and the other the interviewee. When first beginning to use this structure, sample questions can be modeled or provided to give the students some guidance and direction. For example, if the topic is having a pet, the teacher might model questions such as, "What kind of pets do you have?" "What do you do to take care of your pet?" "Has your pet ever been lost?" For Step 2, the students reverse roles. During Step 3, the students RoundRobin, each team member sharing, in turn, what they learned from their partner.

Varied Group Size

For a group of three, each step becomes a separate interview. During each step, two team members interview the third team member, rotating so that everyone has a turn to be interviewed. With groups of five, two of the students pair and function as one student.

Interview Content

The content of an interview can be anything. It can be used to have students relate personal experiences, to preview knowledge the student may have about a topic, to help students become personally involved in a topic, and to review what a student has learned from a unit of study. Because its strength in having students relate personal experiences, it works great as a anticipatory set to a lesson.

Three-Step Interview

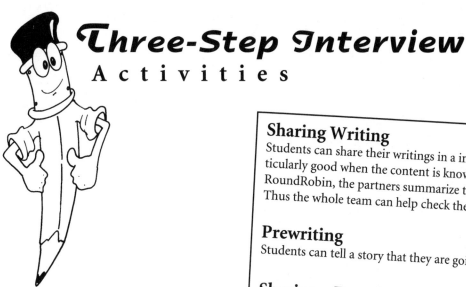

Three-Step Interview
A c t i v i t i e s

Sharing Writing
Students can share their writings in a interview structure. This is particularly good when the content is knowledge-based. In Step 3, the RoundRobin, the partners summarize the information that they heard. Thus the whole team can help check the information for accuracy.

Prewriting
Students can tell a story that they are going to write.

Sharing a Favorite...
Students can share a favorite poem, book, author, story, play.

Retell a Story
Students can retell the story they are studying in preparation for making a story map.

Value Statements
Given a topic, students create a value statement that tells how they feel about the issue and then share the statement and its meaning during the interview.

Relating Personal Experiences
Students can interview each other to find out what personal experiences they have that relate to the topic being studied. This can happen just one time or in a series of interviews. For example, in studying about moving and the change in creates: If you could move anywhere you wanted, where would you move? Have you ever moved? What feelings did you have about moving? What were the best and the worst parts of moving?

Role Play
Students can role play one of the characters in a book (story).

Favorite Book Parts
Students can share favorite parts of a book (story) — favorite action, favorite character.

Story Elements
Students can interview each other on the importance they attach to the elements in a particular book (story). Why was the story set in the country rather than the city? Why do you think the author made Templeton, the rat, such an obnoxious character?

Practicing Grammar
The interview can be set to practice a particular grammatical structure. To enhance the study of future tense, "What will you be doing during your vacation?" To enhance the study of adjectives, "Think of your favorite toy or special belonging. Describe it well enough that your partner could draw it."

Vocabulary
Students can share one or two vocabulary words that were new to them, their meanings, and their context in the book (story).

Relating Common Experiences
Each student shares an experience similar to one that was read about.

Predicting
Students ask, "What do you think the story will be about? What do you think might happen next?"

Writing Structures

Partner Editing

*You can find **Writing Structures** in Lessons 5, 7, 11, 12, 14, 17, 20, 23*

Fastwriting

Fastwriting is a time when students write as quickly as they can without stopping for a given period of time. For first experiences with fastwriting, the time period should be relatively short (three to five minutes). As the students have more experience, the time periods for writing can be lengthened.

Fastwriting allows students the opportunity to capture images and ideas on paper without any regard for correctness. It is a great way to build fluency for writers. It might help students to have them understand that fastwriting is a rehearsal before the actual writing.

Guided Imagery

This structure helps students visualize before writing. By having students close their eyes and concentrate, they can tune out the world around them and focus on the world being created by the Guided Imagery script. A Guided Imagery script slowly leads children, through a series of questions, to discover the topic with their senses and their feelings. The script should help them create images that they can later record on paper during a fastwrite or an independent writing.

Guided Imagery is usually used during the Prewriting stage of the writing process. It helps students collect and focus their ideas. During the Revision stage, imagery can give students input to use in adding to or changing their writing. If a student has asked a question about something in the writing and the writer is unsure how to make any changes, the writer can take a few moments to close his or her eyes and concentrate on the image he or she wants to create.

Partner Editing

In Partner Editing, students working in pairs coach each other, while editing their writing for Punctuation, Capitalization and Spelling. This coaching occurs in three rounds:

Punctuation Round

The teachers read a student writing sample to the class (one that matches the assignment at hand) without pausing to take breaths. Ask the students what they noticed while you were reading. Usually they will say that you didn't stop or slow down while you were reading. Discuss how students can hear the punctuation needed in a poem or story by listening to it as it is read aloud. When the reader pauses to take a breath, a period is needed. When there is a slight pause, a comma is needed. Read the student writing sample to the class again. Have the students listen for the pauses as you read. If they hear a long pause, they raise their hand (Optional for upper grades — and if they hear a short pause they show thumbs up). As the teacher reads, exaggerate the pauses so the students can respond. Tell the students that they will now do the same thing with their own writing. As partner #1 reads orally, he or she marks the pauses he or she hears with a period or a comma. Partner #2 stops partner #1 when he or she reads too quickly and doesn't hear the pause

in the writing. When partner #1 finishes, partner #2 reads orally, while partner #1 acts as a coach.

Capitalization Round

Have the class brainstorm where capital letters are needed in the writing assignment being edited. Make a list on the chalkboard. With their partners acting as coaches, the students orally read through their writing, checking for correct capitalization. The students change roles and the other person reads orally to check for correct punctuation, while the first reader acts as a coach.

Spelling Round

To check a paper for spelling, it is most efficient to read the paper backwards. Each student reads his or her paper backwards, starting at the last word and touching each word, as they check word for word towards the beginning of the paper. When coming across an unknown word, or a word they are unsure of, the student circles it and continues on. After both partners have checked their papers, they trade papers and read their partner's paper the same way — word for word backwards, starting at the last word and touching each word. After finishing checking for spelling errors, the students use dictionaries, each other, and the teacher to correct and/or verify the spelling of any marked words.

Teacher's Note: Usually after going through this editing procedure, students will catch 80-85% of their errors. It is important to emphasize the fact that they found their own errors and they won't get a paper back full of corrections.

Writing Structures

Jeanne Stone: *Cooperative Learning & Language Arts: A Multi-Structural Approach*
Kagan Publishing • 1 (800) 933-2667 • www.KaganOnline.com

Multi-Structural Language Arts Lessons

The following section consists of detailed lesson plans for teaching specific language arts objectives using multiple cooperative learning structures. Each multi-structural lesson flows from structure to structure, building on the previous part of the lesson for specific academic outcomes. The multi-structural approach is powerful, because it provides a high degree of student interaction from the introduction to the closure of a lesson.

In Part II of this book, each structure is explained, along with ideas for using the structure in isolated language arts activities. The ultimate goal in the structural approach, however, is to provide the teacher with the ability to link structures together to make complete lessons.

These multi-structural language arts lessons are written as models for teachers to use in planning lessons for all language arts objectives. With experience, teachers will know which structures are best for concept development and which are best for practice, along with the appropriate sequencing of structures from the beginning to the end of a lesson. The structures will also help focus the students' listening and speaking skills while strengthening their reading and writing skills.

Each lesson features an Overview that includes the domain of writing, the academic skills involved, the cooperative learning structures used, the materials needed, and an estimate of the time it will take to complete the lesson. The suggested grade levels are under the title. Following the Overview are the step-by-step instructions for each structure in the lesson. Blackline masters of the handouts are included at the end of each lesson.

To enhance the delivery of multi-structural language arts lessons, it is recommended that teachers preview the steps for each structure, so that clear directions may be given to the students.

Above all else, it is hoped that teachers and students will enjoy language arts through cooperative learning and the multi-structural approach.

Part III

Time for a Rhyme

Grades K - 2

Lesson-At-A-Glance

Domain:
Sensory/Descriptive

Academic Skill:
Listening: Listen to rhymes
Speaking: Use rhythm in retelling a rhyme
Reading: Memorize a rhyme
Writing: Rewrite a rhyme

Structures:
- *Within-Team Jigsaw*
- *Corners*
- *Class Brainstorming*
- *RoundRobin*
- *Independent Writing*

Materials:
- One, Two, Buckle My Shoe Chart
- Teaching Steps chart
- Writing a Poem handout
- Rhyme handouts
- Small piece of paper

Time:
1-2 language arts periods

Teacher's Note: When this lesson is done in Kindergarten, all the activities can be done orally.

Lesson Overview

The students become "teachers," something they love to do. Each team member learns a rhyme to go back and teach their teammates. After learning the rhymes, the students use one as a pattern in writing their own version of the rhyme.

Lesson Sequence

1 How to teach a rhyme using *Modeling*

Explain to the students that they will become teachers. They will each learn a rhyme to teach to their teammates.

Post a chart with the rhyme "One, Two, Buckle My Shoe." Using it, model how the students will teach a new rhyme to their teammates. Post a **Teaching Steps** chart (see handout) for the students to refer to throughout the lesson.

1. The teacher reads the rhyme aloud.
2. The teacher and the students clap the rhythm while the teacher is reading (saying) the rhythm. (This needs to be done a few times to make sure the students are clapping the rhythm correctly.)
3. The students and the teacher read (say) the rhyme together.
4. The students read (say) the rhyme alone.

While teaching the rhyme, reinforce the teaching steps with the students so that they will be comfortable using them when they are the teacher.

2 Learning a rhyme using *Within-Team Jigsaw*

The team members number off 1, 2, 3, 4. Each of the students goes to a corner to learn a rhyme.

1 - "It's Raining, It's Pouring"
2 - "Rain on the Green Grass"
3 - "If Bees Stay at Home"
4 - "Rain, Rain, Go Away"

While the students are learning the rhymes in their corners, reinforce the teaching steps that the students will use.

When all the students have learned their rhymes, they return to their teams to do a RoundRobin to teach each other their rhymes. They use the teaching steps on the Teaching Steps chart.

Teacher's Note: The logistics of this lesson vary depending on the number of "master" teachers that will be available. The easiest way to approach this lesson is to have four upper grade students come to the classroom to teach the rhymes, while the teacher monitors. These students should be trained ahead of time so that they understand the teaching steps that will be used. With one or two master teachers, have some of the group(s) go to the corner(s), while the others are at their seats illustrating their rhymes on the Rhyme handouts.

When all rhymes have been taught, have the class review the rhymes by saying them all together.

3 Picking a favorite rhyme using *Corners*

Write the name of each rhyme on a different color paper. Mount each sign in a different area of the room. Have the students pick one of the new rhymes they liked and color a small piece of paper to match the sign. Then have them go to the matching sign. Within their corners, have the students pair up, clap, and say their rhymes. Have them pick a new partner to clap and say the rhyme again.

The students pick a different rhyme and go to the new corner. Within the corners, have the students pair up, say, and clap their rhymes. Have them pick a new partner, say, and clap the rhyme again.

This step can be repeated two more times to give the students the opportunity to practice all the rhymes.

The students return to their seats.

4 Listing where rain falls using *Class Brainstorming*

Tell the students that they will be rewriting one of the rhymes that they have just learned, to make a new rhyme of their own.

Have the students say the rhyme "Rain on the Green Grass." Ask the students to think about other places that rain can fall. Remind the students of their numbers: 1, 2, 3, and 4. Tell the students that each number will have a chance to respond during the Class Brainstorming.

Lesson 1

Jeanne Stone: *Cooperative Learning & Language Arts: A Multi-Structural Approach*
Kagan Publishing • 1 (800) 933-2667 • www.KaganOnline.com

As a number is called, anyone with that number can give an idea for where rain can fall. #1 is called, and their ideas are recorded on the class chart. #2 is called, then #3 and finally #4. After all the numbers have had a chance to have their ideas recorded, the brainstorming returns to a free-for-all for any remaining ideas.

Teacher's Note: Though it takes a few minutes longer, calling each number to sit in front of the Class Chart as they respond keeps students focused and involved.

5 Completing a rhyme using *RoundRobin*

Have each student select three ideas from the brainstorming list, and draw them on separate pieces of paper. The ideas can be repeated among team members if the team members choose the same idea.

Model for the students how they can use their pictures to say a new rhyme.

"Rain on the _____

Rain on the _____

Rain on the _____

But not on me!"

Have the students RoundRobin their own version of "Rain on the Green Grass" with their teammates.

6 Writing a poem using *Independent Writing*

Pass out the **Writing A Poem** handout. Students complete the handout using either words or pictures.

These can be bound into a class book for the class library.

Theme Rhymes

Cats
Three Little Kittens
As I Was Going to St. Ives
Pussy Cat, Pussy Cat
Cat Goes Fiddle-i-fee
Hey Diddle, Diddle
I Love Little Pussy

Food
Simple Simon
Sing a Song of Sixpence
Hot Cross Buns

Bugs
Little Miss Muffet
Eency, Weency Spider
Ladybird, Ladybird

Pigs
This Little Pig Went to Market
Tom, Tom the Piper's Son
To Market, To Market

Sheep and Cows
Little Bo Peep
Mary Had a Little Lamb
Little Boy Blue
Baa, Baa, Black Sheep
Hey Diddle, Diddle

Jack
Jack Be Nimble
Jack and Jill
Jack Sprat
See-saw Margery Daw
Little Jack Horner

Numbers
One, Two, Buckle My Shoe
One, Two, Three, Four, Five
Ten Little Indians

Available in *Tomie dePaola's Mother Goose* published by G.P. Putnam's Sons, New York, 1985.

Lesson 1

Extensions

Sharing Rhymes
Use Inside-Outside Circle for the students to share their completed rhymes with their classmates.

New Copy Change
Make other Writing handouts to use for copy-change activities with the other poems.

Changing the Theme
Repeat this lesson using other nursery rhymes, short poems, or finger plays grouped by theme. See the Theme Rhymes box on the previous page.

Lesson 1

Jeanne Stone: *Cooperative Learning & Language Arts: A Multi-Structural Approach*
Kagan Publishing • 1 (800) 933-2667 • www.KaganOnline.com

102

Teaching Steps

1 The teacher reads the rhyme aloud.

2 The teacher and students clap the rhythm while the teacher is reading the rhythm.

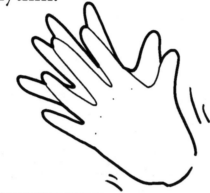

3 The students and teacher read rhyme together.

4 The students read the rhyme alone.

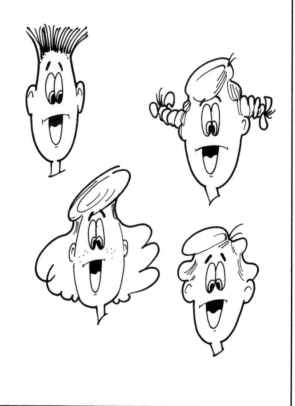

Lesson 1

Jeanne Stone: *Cooperative Learning & Language Arts: A Multi-Structural Approach*
Kagan Publishing • 1 (800) 933-2667 • www.KaganOnline.com

103

Writing a Poem

Rain on the _____,

And rain on the _____,

Rain on the _____,

But not on me.

Jeanne Stone: *Cooperative Learning & Language Arts: A Multi-Structural Approach*
Kagan Publishing • 1 (800) 933-2667 • www.KaganOnline.com

Draw a picture for the rhyme.

It's raining, it's pouring,

The old man is snoring;

He got into bed,

And bumped his head,

And couldn't get up in the morning.

Lesson 1

Jeanne Stone: *Cooperative Learning & Language Arts: A Multi-Structural Approach*
Kagan Publishing • 1 (800) 933-2667 • www.KaganOnline.com

105

Draw a picture for the rhyme.

Rain on the green grass,

And rain on the tree,

Rain on the housetop,

But not on me.

Jeanne Stone: *Cooperative Learning & Language Arts: A Multi-Structural Approach*
Kagan Publishing • 1 (800) 933-2667 • www.KaganOnline.com

Draw a picture for the rhyme.

If bees stay at home,

Rain will soon come;

If they fly away,

Fine will be the day.

Lesson 1

Jeanne Stone: *Cooperative Learning & Language Arts: A Multi-Structural Approach*
Kagan Publishing • 1 (800) 933-2667 • www.KaganOnline.com 107

Draw a picture for the rhyme.

Rain, rain, go away,

Come again another day,

Little Johnny wants to play.

Rain, rain, go to Spain,

Never show your face again.

Jeanne Stone: *Cooperative Learning & Language Arts: A Multi-Structural Approach*
Kagan Publishing • 1 (800) 933-2667 • www.KaganOnline.com

Animal Riddles

Grades 2 - 3

Lesson-At-A-Glance

Domain:
Sensory/Descriptive

Academic Skill:

Listening:	Listen to paraphrase
Speaking:	Paraphrase what was said
	Participate in group discuss
Reading:	Categorize words
Writing:	Write a riddle, use adjectives

Structures:
- *Think-Pair-Share*
- *Similarity Groups*
- *Three-Step Interview*
- *Numbered Heads Together*
- *Brainstorming*
- *Unstructured Sort*
- *Team Discussion*
- *Simultaneous RoundTable*
- *Independent Writing*
- *Two-Box Induction*

Materials:
- 1 Riddle Page handout per team
- Sentence with Adjectives handout
- Pictures of lions (or another well-known animal)
- 1 Sentence strip per team
- Examples of statements & questions
- Transparency (optional)

Time:
1-2 language arts periods

Lesson Overview

Students' love of riddles and animals combine to reinforce the concept of adjectives. Students select their favorite animal and find others who like the same animal. After review and practice with adjectives, the students write a class riddle. Finally, each student writes a riddle about his/her favorite animal.

Lesson Sequence

1 Naming favorite animals using *Think-Pair-Share*

Say to the students, "Today we're going to be talking about animals. How many of you like animals? Think of your favorite animal." (Pause.) "Close your eyes. What does it look like? Where is it? What does it do? Pair up and tell your partner about your favorite animal."

2 *Grouping by* **favorite animal using** *Similarity Groups*

Have each student write the name of their favorite animal on a piece of paper. Students move about the classroom finding others whose favorite animal matches theirs and form groups with all like animals together.

Have the students pair up with the person next to them and talk about why they like that animal. They should include one or two specific details about the animal

(It's large and furry.) and they should tell about something it likes to do (It always barks at the mailman.) The students pair up and share again. Within each group, the pairs pair and RoundRobin.

A student from one similarity group shares with the other groups what animal the group likes and why his or her group likes that particular animal. Someone in one of the other groups paraphrases something that was shared by the first group and then shares something his or her group said. Continue until all groups have had an opportunity to share.

 **Teacher's Note:** If students are adept at paraphrasing, have them paraphrase with a partner in their group rather than with the whole class.

The students return to their teams.

3 **Observing differences in words using *Two Box Induction* with *Think-Pair-Share***

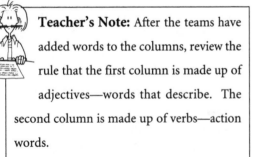 **Teacher's Note:** After the teams have added words to the columns, review the rule that the first column is made up of adjectives—words that describe. The second column is made up of verbs—action words.

Make a chart with two columns. Write a descriptive word (adjective) in the first column and a verb in the second column.

| _____ | _____ |
| brown | fly |

Ask the students to think about the words on the lists. Have them pair up and discuss how the two words are different. Add an adjective to the first column.

_____	_____
brown	fly
quiet	

Have the students look at the two words in the first column and think about how they are the same. Students pair up to discuss what rule might be used to describe the words in the first column. Have those that want to, share their rule with the class and write them on the chalkboard.

Then add a verb to the second column.

_____	_____
brown	fly
quiet	sing

The students look at the two words in the second column and think about how they are the same. Again they pair up to discuss what rule might be used to describe the words in the second column and how they are different from the words in the first column. Have students share some of their ideas with the class.

The teacher then adds another word to each column.

_____	_____
brown	fly
quiet	sing
tiny	build

The students again Think-Pair-Share about the rules for each column and give sample words to try out their rule. The process continues until most of the students have had a chance to successfully add to one of the columns.

Jeanne Stone: *Cooperative Learning & Language Arts: A Multi-Structural Approach*
Kagan Publishing • 1 (800) 933-2667 • www.KaganOnline.com

4 Naming the rule using *Three-Step Interview*

In pairs, have the students interview each other about what rule is used to place the words in the columns. RoundRobin.

Ask the students, "Is there any team that agrees on what the rule is and can share the rule with the class?" Have the teams share their rule, and with teacher monitoring, add one word to each list.

5 Practicing with adjectives using *Numbered Heads Together*

 Teacher's Note: Spend enough time on each round, so that the students are fairly fluent in their answers.

Round One: Show the students a Round One sentence from the **Sentences with Adjectives** handout.

> **The dog is <u>brown</u>.**

The students put their heads together to decide if the underlined word is an adjective or not. The team members that respond can respond with a Thumbs Up for adjectives and a Thumbs Down for words that are not adjectives.

Round Two: Show the students a Round Two sentence from the Sentences with Adjectives handout.

> **The green grass grows all around the tree.**

The students put their heads together. Ask, "What is the adjective in this sentence?"

Round Three: Students put their heads together to be able to name an adjective.

This can be made easier by giving the students a subject to describe — "Name an adjective describing an elephant."

6 Listing words to describe a lion using *Brainstorming*

Pass out pictures of lions (or another common animal). Students brainstorm words that describe a lion (or another common animal) and its actions.

7 Sorting words using *Unstructured Sort*

Students categorize the words they have brainstormed. While monitoring the students, encourage them to make a category for words that describe lions (or another common animal) and words that tell what lions do (verbs).

8 Making a team sentence using *Team Discussion*

Students share the Riddle Page handout at their table. Tell the students that they will all help to write a riddle about a lion.

Each team comes up with a sentence using two or three of the words from the Brainstorming and Unstructured Sort. Each team records their sentence on sentence strips. All the sentence strips are then displayed one under another on the wall or in a pocket chart. Have each team read their sentence to the class. Lead the students in a discussion as to which sentence makes a good beginning. Continue until the clues have been placed in order and are finished with a "What is it?" All the sentences together make a class riddle about a lion.

Lesson 2

Jeanne Stone: *Cooperative Learning & Language Arts: A Multi-Structural Approach*
Kagan Publishing • 1 (800) 933-2667 • www.KaganOnline.com   111

9 Listing words to describe animals using *Simultaneous RoundTable*

Each student puts the name of an animal (their favorite animal or any other) at the top of a piece of paper. Encourage the students to think of different animals than their teammates. The papers are

Teacher's Note: Each sentence can be recorded on a Teeny Tiny Transparency, a small strip of transparency. They can be lined up one under the other on an overhead.

folded in half vertically. As the papers are passed in Simultaneous RoundTable, the students add adjectives to the left hand column or verbs in the right hand column to describe each animal listed at the top of each page.

10 Writing a riddle using *Independent Writing*

Students use the adjectives and verbs on their lists to write a riddle about his or their animal.

11 Sharing riddles using *Three-Step Interview*

Within the team, each student has a partner. Students read their riddle to their partners. The partners respond with the name of the animal and what part of the riddle they like best. The roles are reversed and the sharing repeated. Students RoundRobin by telling the best part of the riddle they heard. If the part-

ners could not guess the riddle, following the RoundRobin the team can give suggestions on ways to revise the riddle and make it clearer. The riddles can be revised for homework and published in a class animal riddle book.

Theme Riddle Books
Have the students create a variety of theme riddle books. These can either be class-created books, with each student contributing one riddle, or team-created books with each member of the team writing several riddles. Some possible themes:
  Dinosaurs
  Food
  Favorite People
  Around the School
  Favorite Tales
  Into the Trash (common throw-away items)
  Holiday Characters: Halloween, Christmas, Thanksgiving, Easter

Riddle books abound, but these are a few of my favorites:
It Does Not Say Meow by Beatrice Schenk de Regniers
Q Is For Duck by Mary Elting and Michael Folsom

Lesson 2

Riddle Page

I'm small and furry.
I like to lay in the warm sun.
I purr when I'm happy and screech when I'm angry.
What am I? (*a cat*)

Deep in the jungle I roam hunting for food.
I creep as quietly as a cat.
My stripes are black.
What am I? (*a tiger*)

Down on the farm is my home sweet home.
I spend much of my time just sitting around.
I like to peck for corn and wheat the farmer throws me.
What am I? (*a chicken*)

I can fly as high as the sky.
I sing sweetly in the morning.
Worms and grub are my favorite foods.
What am I? (*a bird*)

My black and white stripes make me look like a convict.
I travel over grasslands.
I can run fast to escape from my enemies.
What am I? (*a zebra*)

For other riddles see,
It Does Not Say Meow and Other Animal Riddle Rhymes by Beatrice Schenk de Regniers

Lesson 2

Sentences with Adjectives

Round One

The <u>old</u> woman walked home.

<u>Red</u> apples grow on the tree.

The woman lives in a <u>tiny</u> cottage.

The house has a <u>small</u> window.

The apples are <u>shiny</u>.

The woman puts on a <u>pink</u> bonnet.

She walks down a <u>long</u> road.

She looks for <u>yellow</u> daisies to pick.

<u>Brown</u> rabbits hop by.

She puts the <u>pretty</u> flowers on her table.

Round Two

Two girls went walking in the woods.

They saw many bugs.

Some were pretty butterflies.

Others were crawling beetles.

They collected some of the multicolored bugs to take home.

At home they put them in glass jars.

The ladybug was red with black spots.

The beetle was reddish brown.

The butterfly was orange and black.

The grasshopper was long and green.

Lesson 2

Jeanne Stone: *Cooperative Learning & Language Arts: A Multi-Structural Approach*
Kagan Publishing • 1 (800) 933-2667 • www.KaganOnline.com

What Shall I Wear?

Grades 2 - 6

Lesson-At-A-Glance

Domain:
Sensory/Descriptive
Imaginative/Narrative
Practical/Informative
Analytical/Expository

Academic Skill:

Listening:	Listen to student presentations
Speaking:	Participate in a choral reading
Reading:	(Varied depending on the material chosen)
	Create a story map
	Retell a story
	Summarize a story
	Prepare a choral reading
Writing:	Write a poem, story, or report about clothing

Structures:
- *Class Project*
- *Team Discussion*
- *Co-op Co-op*
- *Corners*
- *Independent Writing*
- *RoundRobin*

Materials:
- A variety of books and poems about clothing (see Resource List)-at least one selection per team
- "Winter Clothes" by Karla Kuskin (p. 128 in *Random House Book of Poetry for Children*) or other clothing poem
- Team Performance Handout
- Resource List handout for other topics

Time:
2 or 3 language arts periods

Lesson Overview

"What Shall I Wear?" provides an example of exploring a thematic unit with a multi-structural lesson. Students explore a wide variety of literature about clothing. Each team is responsible for selecting a book, story, or poem about clothing and presenting it to the class. After the team presentations, each student writes a response based on the presentations. Included in the lesson are resource lists to use the same lesson with themes of friendship, bears, and brothers and sisters.

This lesson frame can be used with many different thematic ideas. Included at the end of this lesson are thematic book lists that could be inserted into this multi-structural lesson.

Lesson Sequence

1 Choral reading using *Class Project*

Pass out copies of "Wendy in Winter" or another clothing poem to the class. Have the class listen as the teacher reads it. Have everyone read it with the teacher. Assign specific lines to different teams, to the boys, or to the girls. Read the poem again with everyone reading their assigned lines. Practice a few times so that the final reading can be a choral speaking "performance."

Options

1. The final "performance" can be taped for the class to enjoy later.
2. The choral reading of "Wendy in Winter" can be enhanced if someone is acting out the poem as it is recited.

2 Discussing clothing in their lives using *Team Discussion*

Ask the teams to discuss the role that clothing has in their lives. Some sample questions may be:

Is clothing important?

Is clothing something people need or want or both?

How does your clothing affect the people around you?

What can you learn from someone's clothing?

Is clothing seasonal? In what way and where?

Tell the students that the teams are going to look at a variety of readings on clothing and share them with the class. After hearing many different stories, poems, and reports on clothing, each student will record some of his or her own ideas about clothing in a poem, story, or report.

3 Creating a team presentation on clothing using *Co-op Co-op*

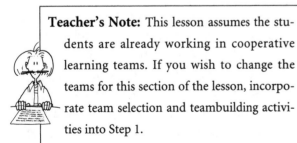

Teacher's Note: This lesson assumes the students are already working in cooperative learning teams. If you wish to change the teams for this section of the lesson, incorporate team selection and teambuilding activities into Step 1.

Step 1: Students participate in a class discussion that previews the books and poems that will be looked at during the lesson. The teacher can present the materials to the students or can set up a Gallery Tour so that the students have an opportunity to look at all or most of the materials that they can select from.

Step 2: Each team selects a book or poem about clothing.

Step 3: Each team works together to read and discuss the material that they have selected.

Step 4: Each team decides on what kind of presentation they will do. Some examples might be: to reenact a story, to prepare a choral reading of a poem, to make story boards, to create a story map with alternate endings, to act out a scene from the story, to do a Reader's Theater of the story. The teams prepare their presentation. Each team member is involved in the preparation of the presentation and is in the presentation to the class.

Step 5: Each team presents to the class. The presentations can be in a variety of formats.

• **Team Reports.** Teams are given a time limit and present one at a time.

• **Team Inside-Outside Circle.** Each team faces another team. The inside team presents to the outside team (with a time limit). The outside team gives RoundRobin appreciation. The outside team presents followed by RoundRobin appreciation from the inside team. The teams have a improvement period before they rotate and the process is repeated.

Lesson 3

Step 6: Evaluation – Each team can be evaluated on how well they presented the main ideas of the material that they were responsible for. The teachers and the students may collaborate on the evaluation. See a sample evaluation form on the **Team Performance** handout.

4 Writing about clothing using *Independent Writing*

After all the team presentations, each student writes his or her own response to clothing.

The materials used to prepare the presentation can be set up in a resource area for the students to review as they begin their independent writing. Some sample topics are:

Grades 2 and 3

*   Write a story about getting dressed for a _____ day.

type of weather
*   Write a variation on one of the stories shared in the class (*The Mitten* by Jan Brett for example).
*   Write a news report about Bartholomew's 500 hats.
*   Make a chart explaining the steps in making wool clothing (from sheep to coat).
*   Write a poem about a favorite article of clothing — flowered shorts, a ragged shirt, a dirty hat, holey tennis shoes, etc.
*   Write some new pages for *Animals Should Definitely Not Wear Clothing*.

Grades 4 to 6

*   Write a recipe for dressing for a _____ day.

type of weather

*   Write an adventure that could happen in winter. Include all the clothes that help you survive.
*   Write a story about losing _____ and what happened to it.
*   Pretend to be a former classmate and write a letter to Wanda (The Hundred Dresses).
*   Write a news report about the emperor's walk in his new "clothes".
*   Black paint was spilled on your father's new tennis shoes. Write about how the paint got there and what possible solutions there might be.
*   Prepare a clothing manual that illustrates and describes the dress for a variety of social settings: school, church, play, beach, party, etc. This might be a team or small group writing activity.
*   Write a letter to a parent convincing him/her that is okay to wear a bathing suit to a beach party in December.

5 Grouping by the domain of writing using *Corners*

When the writing is complete, have the students reread their writing and choose the domain of writing it represents:
Sensory/Descriptive (a poem, a diary entry, a description);
Imaginative/Narrative (a narrative story);
Practical/Informative (a recipe, a news article, a manual); or
Analytical/Expository (problem and solution, persuasion, compare/contrast).
Post a writing domain sign in four corners of the room and have the students go to the corner for the type of writing they did.

Lesson 3

6 Forming new teams using *Corners*

Within the corners, have the students form teams of four or five to share their writing. Each new "team" sits down together. For teambuilding, they quickly RoundRobin telling about their favorite article of clothing and why ("I love my blue shorts because when I wear them I feel like I'm part of the sky.").

7 Responding to writing using *RoundRobin*

To share their writings, each person reads his or her story to the whole group two times. (Individual copies can be passed out to each person if the student or teacher has had copies made.) Students listen so that they can point to the words and phrases that had an impact on them, summarize what they heard, or tell the writer how they felt when they were listening. Each student then, using RoundRobin, responds to the writing. Examples of comments might be:

• I liked the part when you said "…"
• One thing I learned about you is …
• The main point to me is …
• I felt _____ when you read the story.
• I learned … when I listened to your story.

The Gambit Chips from Lesson 6 may be used to help guide the student responses.

Lesson 3

Team Performance Handout

1. Effective Use of Time

1	2	3	4	5	6	7

| Much time spent without purpose | Got off track frequently | | Did well, once we got our ideas clear | | No wasted effort- stayed on target | |

2. Development of Ideas

1	2	3	4	5	6	7

| Little done to generate ideas | Ideas were imposed on the group by a few | | Friendly session but not creative | | Ideas were encouraged and fully explored | |

3. Ability to Decide Issues

1	2	3	4	5	6	7

| Poor resolution of difference | Let one person rule | | Made compromises to get the job done | | Genuine agreement and support | |

4. Overall Productivity

1	2	3	4	5	6	7

| Did not accom- plish our goal | Barely accom- plished the job | | Just did what we had to | | Held a highly productive session | |

Adapted for: Lee, K., Oakes, J., Cohn, J., Webb, N. & Farivar, S. "Helping behaviors handbook." Los Angeles: Unpublished Manuscript, Graduate School of Education, University of California, Los Angeles, CA. 1885.
Reprinted by permission from Spencer Kagan's book, *Cooperative Learning*, San Juan Capistrano, CA: Kagan Cooperative Learning, 1993.

Lesson 3

Resource List

Clothing

The Emporer's New Clothes by Hans Christian Andersen
Animals Should Definitely Not Wear
Clothing by Judi Barrett
Pele's New Suit by Elsa Beskow
What Can You Do With a Shoe? Beatrice Schenk de Regniers
One Hundred Dresses by Eleanor Estes
Corduroy by Don Freeman
Mary Wore Her Red Dress by Merle Peek
The 500 Hats of Bartholomew Cubbins by Dr. Seuss
Caps for Sale by Esphyr Slobodkina
The Mitten by Alvin Tressalt
Shoes by Elizabeth Winthrop
A New Coat for Anna by Harriet Ziefert

Poems

"Three Little Kittens"
"Winter Clothes" by Karla Kuskin
"The Mitten Song" by Marie Louise Allen
"Jonathan Bing" by Beatrice Curtis Brown
"Wendy in Winter" by Kaye Starbird
"Summer" by Frank Asch
"Good-by My Winter Suit" by N. M. Bodecker

Friendship

Books

Amos and Boris by William Steig
Anna Banana and Me by Lenore Blegvad
Best Friends Steven Kellogg
Besty Tacy by Maud Hart Lovelace
Bridge to Terebitha by Katherine Paterson
Ernest and Celestine by Gabrielle Vincent
Best Friends by Lee Hopkins
Frog and Toad Are Friends by Arnold Lobel
The Hating Book by Charlotte Zolotow
George and Martha by James Marshall
Gentle Ben by Walt Morey
Little Bear by Else Holmelund Minarik
A Boy, a Dog, and a Frog by Mercer Mayer
Morris and Boris by Bernard Wiseman
May I Bring A Friend? by Beatrice Schenk de Regniers
The Pinballs by Betsy Byars
The Secret Garden by Frances Hodgson Burnett
Do You Want to Be My Friend? by Eric Carle
Will I Have A Friend? by Miriam Cohen

Poetry

"Hug O' War" by Shel Silverstein
"Wrestling" by Kathleen Fraser

"Since Hanna Moved Away" by JudithViorst
"In Between" by Rose Cheroff
"Friends" by Janet C. Miller
"With a Friend" by Vivian Gouled

Bears

Books

Winnie-the-Pooh by A. A. Milne
The Three Bears
Deep in the Forest By Brinton Turkle
Ask Mr. Bear by Marjorie Flack
Corduroy by Don Freeman
Little Bear by Else Holmelund Minarik
The Biggest Bear by Lynd Ward
Big Bad Bruce by Bill Peet
Valentine Bears by Eve Bunting
A Bear Called Paddington by Michael Bond
The Happy Lion and the Bear by Louise Fatio
The Honeybee and the Robber by Eric Carle
Blueberries for Sal by Robert McCloskey

Poetry

"Wild Beasts" by Evaleen Stein
"Teddy Bear, Teddy Bear"
"My Teddy Bear" by Marchette
"My Teddy Bear" Margaret Hillert

Brothers & Sisters

Books

Alexander and the Terrible, Horrible, No Good, Very Bad Day by Judith Viorst
All-of-a-Kind Family by Sydnet Taylor
I'll Fix Anthony by Judith Viorst
Where Lilies Bloom by Vera and Bill Cleaver
Worse Than Willie by James Stevenson
Tales of a Fourth Grade Nothing by Judith Viorst
A Baby Sister for Frances by Russell Hoban
Little House on the Prairie (series)by Laura Ingalls Wilder
Peter's Chair by Ezra Jack Keats
Nobody Ever asked Me If I Wanted a Baby Sister by Martha Alexander
Big Sister and Little Sister by Charlotte Zolotow

Poetry

"In Between" by Rose Cheroff
"Sisters" by Muriel Lumsden Sonne
"Brothers" by Muriel Lumsden Sonne

Lesson 3

Jeanne Stone: *Cooperative Learning & Language Arts: A Multi-Structural Approach*
Kagan Publishing • 1 (800) 933-2667 • www.KaganOnline.com

Colors All Around

Grades 2 - 6

Lesson-At-A-Glance

Domain:
Sensory/Descriptive

Academic Skill:
Listening: Listen to follow directions
Speaking: Share feelings
Reading: Relate personal experiences
Writing: Write a poem

Structures:
- *Team Project*
- *Teacher Talk*
- *Three-Step Interview*
- *Similarity Groups*
- *Team Word-Webbing*
- *Corners*
- *Independent Writing*
- *Team Interview*

Materials:
- Old magazines
- White paper (12 x 18) - 1 per team
- Chart paper - 1 per team, one for class recording, and one for rainbow graph
- Markers - 1 per student (a different color for each team member
- Poetry and stories about color (see Resource List)
- Small pieces multi-colored construction paper for rainbow graph
- Sample Color Poems - poster size
- Sample Color Poems handout

Time:
2-3 language arts periods

Lesson Overview
Teams create a rainbow collage and then explore the images and ideas colors bring to mind. Choosing a favorite color, students find others who like the same color and word-web to create as many images and ideas as they can. The color is then showcased in a poem or a story.

Lesson Sequence

1 Make a rainbow collage using *Team Project*

Students in each team number off from 1 to 4. From old magazines, each student cuts out small pieces of colors to use in making a team rainbow. Assign each team member particular colors according to the chart below, or have all the team members look for all the colors and place them in designated piles in the center of the team.

> **#1 - red and orange**
> **#2 - yellow and green**
> **#3 - blue**
> **#4 - purple**

Give each team one large (12 x 18) piece of white paper. One of the team members sketches a rainbow shape on the paper and the team proceeds to use their color pieces to make a primary or secondary rainbow.

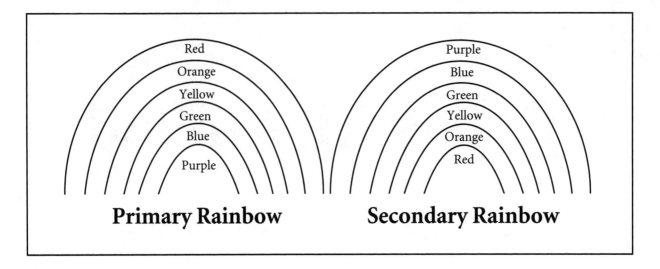

Red
Orange
Yellow
Green
Blue
Purple

Primary Rainbow

Purple
Blue
Green
Yellow
Orange
Red

Secondary Rainbow

When the rainbows are completed, they can be labeled with the team name and posted around the classroom.

2 Listening to Literature **using** *Teacher Talk*

Explain to the students that they are going to continue immersing themselves in color, by collecting ideas, images and emotions.

Read to them (or have them do Paired Reading within their teams) many poems and stories about color, particularly from *Hailstones and Halibut Bones* by Mary O'Neill. Be sure to expose them to a variety of genre.

3 Talking about colors using *Three-Step Interview*

Students use Three-Step Interview to talk about the different kinds of images they saw in the color writings. Have them think and share about the feelings, images, objects, and ideas associated with color. The students can use the **Colors** handout to record ideas they want to remember during RoundRobin part of Three-Step Interview.

With team member #4 acting as the recorder, have two or three responses from each team recorded on class charts for each color. A sample class chart might look like this:

Orange
Objects: ring, cat, carrot.
Feelings: envy, anger, suffering
Images: thunderstorm, evening, a happy day
Sounds: music of the tango, a song, trickling water
Smells: bonfire, Sunday roast

> **Teacher's Note:** Prepare a rainbow-shaped graph on large chart paper. Fold the paper in half and cut in a rainbow shape. Cut small (about 2"x2") pieces of construction paper (red, orange, yellow, green, blue, and purple) for the students to use in marking the graph.

4 Grouping by favorite rainbow colors using *Similarity Groups*

Provide a variety of the small multi-colored pieces of paper for each team. Each student thinks of his or her favorite rain-

Lesson 4

Jeanne Stone: *Cooperative Learning & Language Arts: A Multi-Structural Approach*
122   Kagan Publishing • 1 (800) 933-2667 • www.KaganOnline.com

bow color, and on the count of three, selects a paper of that color.

The students group themselves by colors. Within their color groups, students pair and share why they picked that color. Students switch pairs and share again.

5 Listing words about colors using *Team Word-Webbing*

Students form new teams based on their similarity groups. It is more important for students to remain within the same color group than to have an equal number on each team. Allow teams of three, four, or five to work together for the next part of the lesson. Some colors might be represented by more than one team.

Give each team a piece of chart paper and a different color marker for each member of the team. They are to write the color in the center of the paper and begin word-webbing ideas, thoughts, images and emotions associated with that color. If the teams need more direction, have them use the same categories that were identified during the class charts — objects, feelings, images, sounds, and smells.

Teacher's Note: As the teams are word-webbing, call teams up one at a time to glue their pieces of colored paper on the class rainbow graph in the appropriate color band.

At the completion of the word-webbing, use Teams Consult to have the teams share word-webs with other teams. Encourage them to record comments for each word-web that they look at. Sample comments might be:

Your idea of … helped us think of …
We really liked … because …
Why did you connect … to …?
We don't understand why … made you think of …?

Allow students a few minutes after getting their own word-web back to read the comments from the other teams, and to add any new ideas that they have.

6 Grouping by writing format using *Corners*

In three corners of the room post large samples of different formats for color poems. The fourth corner is blank for the students who want to create their own format. Pass out the **Sample Color Poems** handout. Students review the poem samples and choose one that they want to write. Have the students move to that corner. If they have an idea of their own, they go to the blank corner.

In the corners, students use Paired Reading* to read through the directions for writing the poem they chose. Have them review the directions with their partner. If there is a question while they are reviewing the directions, have them ask another pair. If there is still a question, they can refer back to the directions on the Color Poem Samples handout. Students return to their seats.

*** *Paired Reading*** has students pair up to share the reading responsibility. They can alternate reading sentences, paragraphs, or pages depending on the length of the selection.

7 Writing about colors using *Independent Writing*

Students write a color poem about their chosen color. They should have access to

Lesson 4

the class charts and the word webs that were created earlier in the lesson.

8 Responding to writing using *Team Interview*

The next day, when students have completed their poems, students use Team Interview to share their writings.

Have one student sit in the middle of the team, the student reads his or her poem twice. The other students listen. When the reader is done, the other students make statements or ask questions about his or her color poem. Comments and sharing continue until the teacher gives the signal to move on to the next student.

Resource List

Books

A Rainbow of My Own by Don Freeman
Rain by Robert Kalen
Hailstones and Halibut Bones by Mary O'Neill
Mary Wore Her Red Dress by Merle Peek
Mr. Rabbit and the Lovely Present by Charlotte Zolotow
Red is Best by Kathy Stinson
Who Said Red? by Mary Serfozo

Poems

"Rhinos Purple, Hippos Green" by Michael Patrick Hearn
"Taste of Purple" by Leland B. Jacobs
"The Paint Box" by E. V. Rieu
"What is Pink?" by Christina Rossetti
"Yellow" by David McCord

Lesson 4

Jeanne Stone: *Cooperative Learning & Language Arts: A Multi-Structural Approach*
124   Kagan Publishing • 1 (800) 933-2667 • www.KaganOnline.com

xtensions

Making a Rainbow Book
Rather than having the students write only about one color, they can write about all the colors and make a rainbow book. See the **A Rainbow Book** handout.

My Own Rainbow
After listening to the story, *A Rainbow of My Own* by Don Freeman, have the students write a story about what they would do if they had a rainbow of their own.

A Rainbow Poem
A Rainbow poem is five poems combined into one. Write a poem for each color. First, write three things that are the color. Second, write the color. Third, write how the color makes you feel. Write the poems in a rainbow shape with the color in the center of each arch. See sample poem.

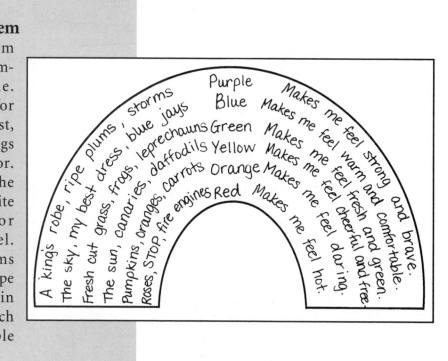

A king's robe, ripe plums, storms Purple Makes me feel strong and brave.
The sky, my best dress, blue jays Blue Makes me feel warm and comfortable.
Fresh cut grass, frogs, leprechauns Green Makes me feel fresh and green.
The sun, canaries, daffodils Yellow Makes me feel cheerful and free.
Pumpkins, oranges, carrots Orange Makes me feel daring.
Roses, STOP, fire engines Red Makes me feel hot.

Lesson 4

Sample Color Poems

Example 1

Directions:

Line 1   Choose a color.
Line 2   Think of some object that is that color.
Line 3   Describe the object again.
Line 4   Name an object that color.
Line 5   Name an object that color.
Line 6   Name an object that color.
Line 7   Write the color as the first word in a sentence.
Line 8   Finish the sentence about the color.

Sample Poem:

Blue
Sky
Far-reaching and clear
Water
A quilt
Spring flowers
Blue
Is the color of a summer evening.

Example 2

Directions:

Line 1   The color
Line 2   Something you see that is that color
Line 3   Something you hear that is that color
Line 4   Something you smell that is that color
Line 5   Something you feel that is that color
Line 6   Something you taste that is that color
Line 7   The color

Sample Poem:

Pink
A new baby's cheeks
The thump of the Easter bunny
A sweet smelling rose
The fuzzy softness of a new blanket
A double-scoop strawberry ice cream cone
Pink

Example 3

Directions:

Write a recipe for a color. List the ingredients. List the mixing directions. Include any additional ideas.

Sample Poem:
A Yellow Day

What you need:
1 basket of sunshine
1 glass of tart lemonade
1 ripe banana
1 summer squash
1 bunch or daffodils
1 egg yolk
1 starry night

What you do:
Mix the sunshine, the daffodils, and the lemonade together.
Now mix in the ripe banana, a summer squash and an egg yolk for a picnic.
At the end of a yellow day, relax and enjoy a starry night.

Lesson 4

Jeanne Stone: *Cooperative Learning & Language Arts: A Multi-Structural Approach*
Kagan Publishing • 1 (800) 933-2667 • www.KaganOnline.com

Colors

Objects: _____
_____
_____
_____

Feelings: _____
_____
_____
_____

Images: _____
_____
_____
_____

Sounds: _____
_____
_____
_____

Smells: _____
_____
_____
_____

Lesson 4

A Rainbow Book

To make a rainbow book, use the pattern below to the make the first page, (red).
For each consecutive page, add 1/2 inch to the bottom of the pattern.
Continue adding the colored pages in order of the rainbow.

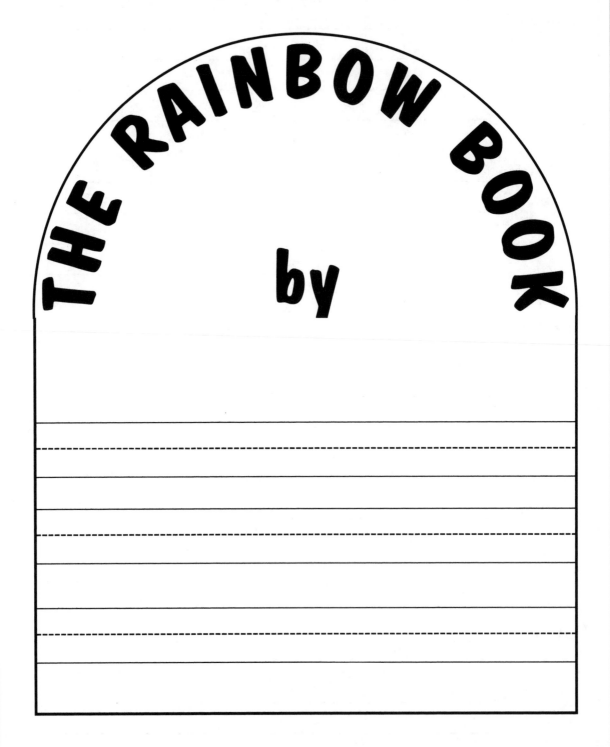

THE RAINBOW BOOK

by

Jeanne Stone: *Cooperative Learning & Language Arts: A Multi-Structural Approach*
Kagan Publishing • 1 (800) 933-2667 • www.KaganOnline.com

Bubbles

Grades 2 - 8

Lesson-At-A-Glance

Domain:
Sensory/Descriptive
Imaginative/Narrative

Academic Skill:
Listening: Listen to follow directions
Speaking: Summarize what was read
Reading: Identify literary genre (poetry, story, non-fiction)
Writing: Write an original story, poem, or non-fiction piece of writing.

Structures:
- *Formations*
- *Line-Ups*
- *Team Project*
- *Team Word-Webbing*
- *Guided Imagery*
- *Fastwrite*
- *Team Discussion*
- *Similarity Groups*
- *Independent Writing*
- *Three-Step Interview*
- *Simultaneous RoundTable*

Materials:
- Bubble solution - Bubbles Resource Sheet
- A wide variety of bubble blowing tools - Bubbles Resource Sheet
- One piece of chart paper for each group.
- Markers - four different colors per team.

Time: 2-3 language arts periods

Lesson Overview
Experiencing an activity is a great precursor to writing and when the activity is something as fun as blowing bubbles, students jump in and get involved. Students have the opportunity to blow bubbles in a variety of ways before collecting their thoughts and ideas to write about bubbles.

Lesson Sequence

1 Shaping bubble blowing tools using *Formations*

Students form various shapes associated with bubble blowing — bubbles, bubble pipe, bubble wand.

2 Counting number of times bubbles have been blown using *Line-Ups*

The teacher says, "Think back through the last year. How many times have you blown bubbles with soap? Line up according to the number of times you have blown bubbles in the last year." Have the students pair up and discuss with the person next to them how they feel about blowing bubbles. Is it something they would like to do more often? Students return to their teams.

3 Blowing bubbles using *Team Project*

Students will blow bubbles with a variety of tools. The teacher assigns the following responsibilities for each team member or allows the students to set their own responsibilities within their teams.

> #1 - **Soap monitor**
> #2 - **Tool monitor**
> #3 - **Clean up monitor**
> #4 - **Gatekeeper**

The assigned students collect the necessary materials and spend five to eight minutes experimenting blowing bubbles. The Gatekeeper makes sure that all students blow bubbles with a variety of tools and that the noise level remains acceptable. Remind students that those tools that touch their mouths should not be shared.

4 Listing words that relate to bubbles using *Team Word-Webbing*

Each team has a sheet of chart paper (or large piece of bulletin board paper.) Each team member has a different colored marker. Starting with the word BUBBLES in a circle in the center of the paper, students quickly RoundTable to create and record the main concepts in ovals around the word BUBBLES.

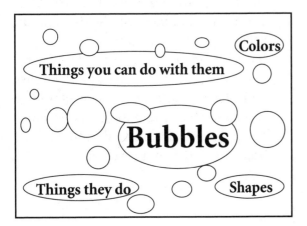

Teacher's Note: The teacher can provide specific categories for the students to use in the Word-Webs if the writing is going to go in a specific direction or if the students need additional guidance to develop ideas about bubbles.

Students then record their ideas about bubbles with each team member using a different color marker. These ideas can be connected as the students go if they wish.

Post the word-webs around the room so that the students can easily refer to them during the rest of the lesson.

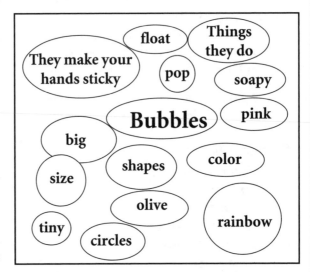

5 Imagining a bubble trip using *Guided Imagery*

Have the students sit comfortably in their seats. Let them know that they will be closing their eyes to think about bubbles and how important it is for them not to disturb the others in the class.

As the teacher reads the Guided Imagery text, it's important to read slowly to allow the students time to develop the mental pictures that will help them with their writing later.

Lesson 5

Guided Imagery

Close your eyes... relax... and focus your attention on your breathing... As you breathe... in and out... relax... Take a deep breath... One... two... three... Feel your body becoming very relaxed... We are going to take an imaginary trip on a transparent bubble... See a picture of a beautiful transparent bubble... very strong... very slick... large enough to hold you... Step into your bubble and gently float away into the sky... Softly whisper it directions as it takes you on a wonderful ride in the sky (pause)... Look all around you... What do you see?(pause)... What can you hear? (pause)... Are there any interesting smells?(pause)... How do you feel to be floating light and free in the air?(pause)... It's time to return to the classroom. Hold onto your ideas as I slowly count to three. One... Two... Three... Take a deep breath and slowly open your eyes... Wiggle your feet and hands... Stretch your arms and legs... Now you will do a fastwrite about your trip on the bubble.

6 Writing about the bubble trip using *Fastwrite*

Each student fastwrites about his or her bubble trip. To fastwrite, students write for a specific amount of time without stopping (usually five to 10 minutes). The idea is for their pencil to never stop moving. If they cannot think of anything to write, they continue writing the last word they wrote over and over again until they get a new idea.

7 Discussing writing genres using *Team Discussion*

Quickly review the bubble activities the students have completed so far. They have been exposed to both descriptive (word webs) and imaginative (guided imagery and fastwrite) prewrites. Have students discuss the genre of writing they can use — poem, tall tale, description, directions for blowing bubbles, etc.

8 Grouping by writing genres using *Similarity Groups*

Students think of the writing genre they will use and write it on a small piece of paper. The students stand up and move about the classroom to find others who are going to use the same genre (poetry, story, non-fiction, informational) that they are going to use. Have the students pair up and discuss what ideas they have for beginning their piece of writing. Pairs pair and do a quick RoundRobin.

9 Writing about bubbles using *Independent Writing*

Students write independently. Suggest that students skip lines to facilitate any changes that they might want to make later.

10 Responding to writing using *Three-Step Interview*

Working in interview pairs, students read their writing to each other. The listener responds about his or her favorite part and the general impact that the content has on him or her. Each partner should also ask a question about a part of the story that he or she was unsure of. During RoundRobin, the students summarize the writing that was read by their partner.

Lesson 5

After the Three-Step Interview is completed, allow time for students to make any changes they wish. Comments and/or questions from team members may give them ideas of changes they might want to make in their writing.

Teacher's Note: Before having your students do this part of the activity, make sure they have participated in a teacher-directed editing lesson that teaches them how to edit papers easily, successfully, and quickly. (See Partner Editing in this book.)

11 Editing writing using *Simultaneous RoundTable*

If the students are ready to move beyond the content of the writing and work with each other on correctness, Simultaneous RoundTable is a quick way for team editing. Each round concentrates on a specific area of correctness:

> Round #1 - Punctuation
> Round #2 - Capitalization
> Round #3 - Spelling
> Round #4 - Sentence Structure

The team's papers are then passed around the group just as in Simultaneous RoundTable. Each person checks each paper for the kind of errors being edited for in that round. After four rounds, the RoundTable stops.

Extensions

Substitute other activities in place of the bubbles and use the same steps of the lesson. Another activity idea is:

Popping Popcorn
For Formations, each team can become a popcorn machine. Replace the Team Projects with an observation of popcorn in different types of machines (oil and hot air). During Guided Imagery students can pretend they are a kernel of corn, and relive the journey from the cob to the popcorn bowl.

Popcorn Book by Tomie de Paola
Popcorn by Frank Asch
What Makes Popcorn Pop? by David Woodside
"Popcorn" by Millicent Selsam

Lesson 5

Bubbles Resource Sheet

Recipe for Basic Bubble Soap
8 tablespoons liquid detergent
1 quart water
Pour the liquid detergent into the quart of water. Stir well to mix.
Note: The thicker (more expensive) liquid detergent seems to work best.

Bubble Windows (bubble blowing tool)
about 20 inches thin string
1 plastic straw (not flexible)

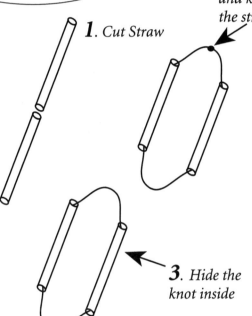

1. Cut Straw

2. Thread and knot the string

3. Hide the knot inside

To make bubbles:
Pour the soap into a flat pan. Holding the a straw in each hand, dip the bubble window into the soap. Starting at waist level, pull up on the bubble window and slowly close the straws together. As the straws touch, the bubble should release. You can also hold the bubble window up and blow through it to release the bubbles.

Tabletop Bubbles
To make Tabletop Bubbles, wet the table top where you want to work. Dip a straw into a glass of soap. Cover the end of the straw and lift out the straw. Move the straw to where you want Tabletop Bubbles. Release the soap onto the table and spread it out. Stick one end of the straw into the soap. Gently blow.

Bubble-Blowing Contraption
Cut the bottom out of a berry basket. Clip a clothespin onto a corner for a handle. Dip the basket into the soap. Blow it or swish it in the air.

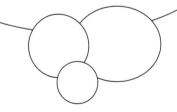

Lesson 5

I Used To...But Now I...

Grades 3 - 6

Lesson-At-A-Glance

Domain:
Sensory/Descriptive

Academic Skill:
Listening: Listening while others are speaking
Speaking: Share a personal experience
Reading: Make inferences
Writing: Write a poem, use capital letters at the beginning of each line of poetry

Structures:
- *Class Brainstorming*
- *Think-Pair-Share*
- *RoundTable*
- *Team Discussion*
- *RoundRobin*
- *Numbered Heads Together*
- *Independent Writing*
- *Inside-Outside Circle*

Materials:
- Magazine pictures - 1 of a baby and 1 of a child about the age of the students
- 2 pieces chart paper
- An example of a poem and an example of a story
- Paper
- I Used to ... But Now I ... handout
- Gambit Chips handout

Time:
1 language arts period

Lesson Overview
Students are fascinated with changes around them and in their lives. This lesson explores what some of those changes are and has students express these changes through poetry.

Lesson Sequence

1 **Listing ideas about pictures using** ***Class Brainstorming***

Have the students number off 1, 2, 3 and 4 on each team. Mount the picture of the baby in one column on the chart paper and the picture of the student in the other column. Starting with the #1's, quickly take ideas that tell what the baby can do and record them under the baby picture on the chart. Continue with the #2's, #3's, and #4's to adding ideas in turn. Repeat the process with the picture of the student, this time starting with the #4's.

Teacher's Note: Hopefully when you are finished, the second column will be noticeably longer than the first column. If not, encourage more responses for the second column.

2 Making inferences about the baby/ student list **using** *Think-Pair-Share*

Ask the students to reread the columns on the chart and think about why there is such a difference in length. Have them pair up and share ideas. After each pair decides on their best idea, have the class do Stand Up and Share. (Every student stands. Starting on one side of the classroom each student shares their idea and then sits down. If a student shares an idea that other students are planning to share later, all students with the same idea sit down. All ideas are shared, but none are repeated.) Record the ideas on a chart paper as they are shared.

> **Teacher's Note:** The students should infer that the second column is longer because the child is older and can do more things. They should understand that change has occurred. If not, you may want to direct their thinking by asking questions similar to the following:
> - How old is the child in column 1? column 2?
> - What is different about the two children?
> - If you had an younger brother or sister, would you be able to do more or less than him or her?
> - If this was the same child, could the pictures have been taken at the same time?
> - What changes have occurred in the children?

3 Listing things the students can do **using** *RoundTable*

Have team member #2 get a piece of paper and a pencil. Tell the students to think about all the things that they can do at school or at home.

The students RoundTable all the things they can do. For example:

    ride a bike
    read a book
    eat lunch
    talk on the telephone
    go to school
    play soccer
    do multiplication facts

4 Discussing the changes in the lists **using** *Team Discussion*

Have each team review their list and discuss the things that they couldn't have done a year ago. Have them underline these things. For example:

    ride a bike
    get dressed
    read a book
    eat lunch
    <u>do multiplication facts</u>
    talk on the telephone
    go to school
    play soccer
    <u>ride a skateboard</u>

Have the students review the list again and circle things they could not have done five or six years ago. For example:

    (ride a bike)
    get dressed
    (read a book)
    eat lunch
    (do multiplication facts)
    (talk on the telephone)
    (go to school)
    play soccer
    (ride a skateboard)

Lesson 6

Jeanne Stone: *Cooperative Learning & Language Arts: A Multi-Structural Approach*
Kagan Publishing • 1 (800) 933-2667 • www.KaganOnline.com

Have the students look at the list and discuss the relationship between the marked and the unmarked items on the list.

With #3 as the reporter, do a quick whip around the classroom. Each team quickly reports the discoveries they made about the list. Compare these discoveries with those charted in the opening exercise.

Teacher's Note: Again, the students should see that as they change and grow bigger and older; there are more and more things that they can do.

5 Creating a team poem using *RoundRobin*

Tell the students that they are going to write a team poem about how things have changed for them.

Have #4 get a piece of paper for each member on the team. Each team member writes and completes this sentence two times:

> I used to _____,
> But now I _____ .

Example:

> **I used to be pushed in a stroller,**
> **But now I can race on my bike.**
> **I used to be eight years old,**
> **But now I am nine.**

Teacher's Note: These sentences can be collected and written as a team poem.

After all the team members have written their sentences, have the students do a RoundRobin to share their ideas.

6 Reviewing poetic structure using *Numbered Heads Together*

Use Numbered Heads Together to do a quick review for the rules for writing poetry. Show students an example of a poem and an example of a story. Ask them questions such as:

- Look at the poem. Do the lines look short or long?
- Look at the story. Do the lines look short or long?
- Tell me two differences between a poem and a story.
- What is needed at the beginning of each line of poetry?
- Does a period go at the end of every line? Why or why not?

7 Writing a poem using *Independent Writing*

The students will write a poem about the changes that have occurred in their lives. This structure is the same as they used in their team poem earlier. (A handout is available.)

> I used to _____,
> But now I _____ .
>
> I used to _____,
> But now I _____ .

They may repeat the basic two-line structure as often as they wish. If they wish to use their own poetry form when writing about the changes they see as they grow, encourage them to do so.

Lesson 6

8 Responding to writing using *Inside-Outside Circle*

After students have finished their poems, pass out a **Gambit Chips** handout to each team. Teams cut the gambit chips apart on the dotted lines. Each student will carry a gambit chip to the Inside-Outside Circle. Have the students form two, equal concentric circles. The inside circle faces out and the outside circle faces in. Each time they rotate the circles, the students share their poems with their partners. The listeners use the gambit chips to give positive feedback to the authors. The gambit chips are:

I like the part when you said ...

When you said ..., it reminded me of ...

Tell me more about ...

To me, the main part of your poem is ...

After both partners have shared, the circle is ready to be rotated.

Extensions

Another Poem

The new poem form can be written by stating an object that represents you before and a description of that object. Then pick an object that represents you now and a description of that object. This verse can be repeated as many times as the author wishes. For example:

Directions

I used to be

a _____,

(description)

But now I am

a _____,

(description)

Sample Poem

I used to be

a fish,

Swimming only in a school.

But now I am

a dolphin,

Swimming far and wide.

A Social Skills Application

After students understand the concept of before and after, have them use the same format to write about a historical event and the effects it had. Students RoundTable the way things were at a specific time in history and then use Team Discussion to mark those items that were different five or ten (or ?) years ago and what could have caused those changes.

Lesson 6

Jeanne Stone: *Cooperative Learning & Language Arts: A Multi-Structural Approach*

Kagan Publishing • 1 (800) 933-2667 • www.KaganOnline.com

I Used to... But Now I...

I used to _____,

But now I _____.

I used to _____,

But now I _____.

I used to _____,

But now I _____.

I used to _____,

But now I _____.

I used to _____,

But now I _____.

I used to _____,

But now I _____.

Lesson 6

Gambit Chips

I like the part when you said...

When you said... it reminded me of...

Tell me more about...

To me, the main part of your poem is...

Jeanne Stone: *Cooperative Learning & Language Arts: A Multi-Structural Approach*
Kagan Publishing • 1 (800) 933-2667 • www.KaganOnline.com

140

I Meant To Do My Work Today

Grades 3 - 8

Lesson-At-A-Glance

Domain:
Sensory/Descriptive

Academic Skill:
Listening: Listen to others share
Speaking: Participate in a discussion
Writing: Write a poem

Structures:
- *RoundTable*
- *Team Discussion*
- *RoundRobin*
- *Independent Writing*
- *Inside-Outside Circle*
- *Partner Editing*

Materials:
- "I Meant to Do My Work Today" by Richard Le Gallienne
- Chart paper

Time:
1-2 language arts periods

Lesson Overview

Students are a wealth of excuses: I didn't do my homework because ..., I can't clean my room because ..., I will take out the trash when ... This lesson allows students the opportunity to use this natural tendency creatively. Students explore different excuses they have used or thought of and use them to write a poem.

Lesson Sequence

1 Listing jobs or chores and excuses using *RoundTable*

Ask the students what jobs they have to do at school or at home. Some examples to get them started are:
- do homework
- read a book
- pick up trash
- pick up my clothes
- do the dishes

Pass out a sheet of paper to each team and tell them they will have to think of jobs or chores they have. Each team folds a paper in half vertically. Team member #1 labels the first column "Things I Have to Do" and the teams RoundTable the different jobs or responsibilities that they have at school or at home.

Share the poem "I Meant to Do My Work Today" by Richard Le Gallienne with the students. Discuss what you would call a reason for not doing something (excuses). Team member #2 labels the second column "Excuses" and the teams RoundTable different excuses for not doing their work. Some examples of excuses are:
- left my pencil at school
- it's too sunny
- my friends want me to ride bikes with them
- the television is on

Remind students to look at the job list to help them think of more excuses.

2 Creating a class excuse chart using *Team Discussion*

The teams discuss what their favorite excuses are. Team member #3 records the team's favorite excuses (two or three) on a class Excuses chart. Remind students not to repeat excuses that other teams have already listed.

3 Creating a team poem using *RoundRobin*

Share the following frame with the students.

I meant to do my work today
But _____,
And _____,
And _____,
And _____,
So what could I do but laugh
and go?

Using the team's list of excuses, the class's list of excuses and any others they might think of, the students RoundRobin to create a team poem (or two or three). The team reads the first line in chorus and then, beginning with team member #1, each team member completes a line. The team reads the last line in chorus, also. After doing the RoundRobin a few

Teacher's Note: There are a variety of ways for the teams to share their poems. They can be shared orally with each team doing a choral reading. They can be written on chart paper and mounted in the classroom. They can be written on a piece of writing paper and put into a class notebook. Team Inside-Outside Circle can also be used to share the team poems.

times, the team records a final poem to share with the class.

4 Writing a poem using *Independent Writing*

Students write their own version of the poem. Encourage them to extend beyond the six line frame.

5 Responding to writing using *Inside-Outside Circle*

Students take their poems with them to Inside-Outside Circle. After the students are in their concentric circles, the sharing begins. The students face a partner and read their poems. The partner shares what excuse they liked hearing. Give directions for a movement around the circle. For example, "Pass three people to the left." The students move and then share with a new partner. After the students have shared four or five times, the class returns to their seats.

Teacher's Note: The type of responses the students give vary depending on the experience they have had with responding to writing. For other response possibilities see Stage 3 - Responding in Part I of this book.

6 Editing writing using *Partner Editing*

Working in pairs, the students coach each other while editing their poems for Punctuation, Capitalization and Spelling. This coaching occurs in three rounds.

Lesson 7

Punctuation Round

Discuss how students can hear the punctuation needed in a poem or story by listening to it as they read it aloud. When the reader pauses to take a breath, a period is needed. When there is a slight pause, a comma is needed. Read the poem "I Meant to Do My Work Today" to the class. Have them listen for the pauses as you read. If they hear a long pause, they raise their hand and if they hear a short pause they show thumbs up. As you read, exaggerate the pauses so the students can respond. Tell the students that they will now do the same thing with their own poem. Students pair. As partner #1 reads his or her writing orally, he or she marks the pauses he or she hears with a period or a comma. Partner #2 stops partner #1 when he or she reads too quickly and doesn't hear the pause in the writing. When partner #1 finishes, partner #2 reads orally, while partner #1 acts as a coach.

Capitalization Round

Review briefly that in this lesson a capital letter is needed at the beginning of each line of the poem or any place there is a person's name. With their partner acting as a coach, the students orally read through their poem checking for correct capitalization. The students change roles and the other partner reads orally, checking for correct punctuation while the first reader acts as a coach.

Spelling Round

To check a paper for spelling, it is most efficient to read the paper backwards. Each student reads his or her paper backwards, starting at the last word and touching each word as they check word for word towards the beginning of the paper. When coming across a unknown or an unsure word, the student circles it or underlines it and continues on. After both partners have checked their own papers, they trade papers and read their partner's paper the same way — word for word backwards, starting at the last word and touching each word. After finishing checking for spelling errors, the students use dictionaries, each other, and the teacher to correct and/or verify the spelling of any marked words.

Teacher's Note: Usually after going through this editing procedure, students will catch 80-85% of their errors. It is helpful to emphasize the fact that they found their own errors and they won't get a paper back full of corrections.

Lesson 7

I Meant To Do My Work Today

I meant to do my work today

But a brown bird sang in the apple tree,

And a butterfly fluttered across the field,

And all the leaves were calling me.

And the wind went sighing over the land,

Tossing the grasses to and fro,

And a rainbow held out its shining hand —

So what could I do but laugh and go?

- Richard Le Gallienne

Jeanne Stone: *Cooperative Learning & Language Arts: A Multi-Structural Approach*
Kagan Publishing • 1 (800) 933-2667 • www.KaganOnline.com

The Very Busy Spider

Grades K - 1

Lesson-At-A-Glance

Domain:
Imaginative/Narrative

Academic Skill:
Listening: Listen to recall sequence
Speaking: Participate in a role play
Retell a story
Reading: Sequence the events in a story
Writing: Substitute text within a story
(Extension activity)

Structures:
• *Teacher Talk*
• *Simple Projects*
• *Team Discussion*
• *RoundRobin*
• *One Stray*

Materials:
• 1 Animal Pictures handouts (cut apart) per class and per team
• 10 sheets 6" x 9" black paper per group
• 1 white crayon per group
• Crayons
• Glue or paste
• *The Very Busy Spider* by Eric Carle or a storybook with a simple sequence

Time:
1 language arts period

Lesson Overview

Using role play and retelling, students familiarize themselves with the sequence of a story. They then make a team book to use in retelling the story to other teams.

This lesson can be done with any story book with a simple sequence. Use the same steps, but substitute pictures and activities appropriate to the story. This lesson or any variation of it should be prefaced with many previous readings of the book being used.

Lesson Sequence

1 Reviewing the story using *Teacher Talk*

Reread *The Very Busy Spider* by Eric Carle. Encourage the students to join in "reading" the animals' questions and tell what the spider was doing.

Pass out pictures of the animals from the **Animals Pictures** handouts to some of the students. Have those students come to the front of the class and guide them in acting out the story of the very busy spider. Repeat this two or three more times so that all the students have a chance to participate in the role play.

Tell students that they are going to create their own versions of *The Very Busy Spider* for the class library.

2 Making a team book using *Simple Project*

Teacher's Note: Prepare the animal pictures for the Simple Project by copying the **Animal Pictures** handouts for each team. In Kindergarten, it is helpful to cut the pictures apart before the students begin working.

Assign the following roles to the students.
- **Team member #1** - Draws a spider web on each page.
- **Team member #2** - Colors the animals and collects supplies.
- **Team member #3** - Colors the animals and collects supplies.
- **Team member #4** - Glues animals onto each page.

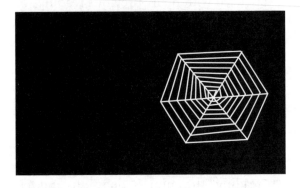

Team member #2 collects ten sheets of 6" x 9" black construction and one white crayon for the team. Team member #3 collects the animal pictures and glue for the team.

When all the materials have been distributed, model how #1 will draw a spider web with the white crayon on the right side of each of the ten black pages.

Team member #1 begins making the spider webs. Team members #2 and #3 begin coloring the animals. As the animals are colored, team member #4 glues one animal picture to the left of each spider web.

3 Sequencing the book using *Team Discussion*

When the pages are complete, the students discuss the correct order in which the animals appear in the story and sequence the pages accordingly. When the pages are in order, the teacher provides a black title page with the title written in white. Each team member signs his or her name on the title page.

The Very Busy Spider

By

Tom, Susan, Jose, and Ana

4 Reading the team book using *RoundRobin*

As the teams wait for the other teams to finish, each team begins "reading" the team book. Each person "reads" one page of the story and the book passes around

Lesson 8

Jeanne Stone: *Cooperative Learning & Language Arts: A Multi-Structural Approach*
Kagan Publishing • 1 (800) 933-2667 • www.KaganOnline.com

146

the team until the story is read. This can be done as many times as necessary until all the teams have finished their books and have had a chance to "read" them.

5 Sharing the team book using *One Stray*

One Stray provides an opportunity for the students to "read" their book to another team. In each of the four rounds, one of the team members travels to another team to "read" his or her team's book to that team.

In Round 1, team member #1 travels with the team's book one team to the right (or left). Team members #2, #3, and #4 stay and listen to the story read to them by the visiting team member #1. After the reading, the team claps, offers a cheer or gives a positive response. All members return to the home teams.

In Round 2, team member #2 travels with the team's book two teams to the right (or left). Team members #1, #3, and #4 stay and listen to the story read to them by the visiting team member #2. After the reading, the team claps, offers a cheer or gives a positive response. All members return to the home teams.

In Round 3, team member #3 travels with the team's book three teams to the right (or left). Team members #1, #2, and #4 stay and listen to the story read to them by the visiting team member #3. After the reading, the team claps, offers a cheer or gives a positive response. All members return to the home teams.

In Round 4, team member #4 travels with the team's book four teams to the right (or left). Team members #1, #2, and #3 stay and listen to the story read to them by the visiting team member #4. After the reading, the team claps, offers a cheer or gives a positive response. All members return to the home teams.

Extension

If students are ready to write independently, this same activity can be done on white paper and they can add the dialogue for each animal. A sample page might look like this:

"Moo, moo," said the cow. "Want to _____?"

The spider didn't answer. She was very busy spinning her web.

Lesson 8

Animal Pictures

Jeanne Stone: *Cooperative Learning & Language Arts: A Multi-Structural Approach*
Kagan Publishing • 1 (800) 933-2667 • www.KaganOnline.com

Animal Pictures

Lesson 8

Jeanne Stone: *Cooperative Learning & Language Arts: A Multi-Structural Approach*
Kagan Publishing • 1 (800) 933-2667 • www.KaganOnline.com   **149**

A Horrible Day!

Grades 2 - 8

Lesson-At-A-Glance

Domain:
Imaginative/Narrative

Academic Skill:

Listening:	Listen to remember what was said
Speaking:	Summarize what was read
Reading:	Relate personal experiences to a story
Writing:	Write an imaginative story Combine sentences

Structures:
- *Think-Pair-Share*
- *RoundTable*
- *Group Discussion*
- *Brainstorming*
- *Unstructured Sort*
- *Simultaneous RoundTable*
- *Independent Writing*
- *RoundRobin*

Materials:
- *Alexander and the Terrible, Horrible, No Good, Very Bad Day* by Judith Viorst
- Sentence Combining handout
- A Horrible Day handout
- Small pads of paper or Post-its
- Chart paper or overhead transparencies

Time:
1-2 language arts periods

Lesson Overview

Students can identify with those days that everything seems to go wrong. The alarm clock didn't go off, the favored shirt is dirty, someone ate all the cereal, and so on through the day. Through the use of Judith Viorst's *Alexander and the Terrible, Horrible, No Good, Very Bad Day*, students will experience someone else's horrible day and then write their own version of what a horrible day would be like for them.

Lesson Sequence

1 **Talking about a horrible day using *Think-Pair-Share***

The teacher asks the students, "Have you ever had a day when things just didn't seem to go right? Think about the things that went wrong that day."

Students pair up with a partner and share some of the things that went wrong that day. Use Stand Up and Share* to have the students share some of their thoughts with the whole class.

Stand-Up and Share: Every student stands. Starting on one side of the classroom each student shares their idea and then sits down. If a student shares an idea that other students are planning to share later, all students with the same idea sit down. All ideas are shared, but none are repeated.

The teacher introduces and reads the book *Alexander and the Terrible, Horrible, No Good, Very Bad Day* to the class. Encourage the students to join in on the chorus "...a terrible, horrible, no good, very bad day."

After the reading, the students think about the story and then share its similarities with their own experiences.

2 Remembering what was read using *RoundTable*

Students RoundTable all the different things that happened to Alexander on his horrible day. Use Post-its or a small pad of paper to record each response on a different sheet of paper.

3 Organizing what happened in the story using *Sorting*

When they are done, have the students review the events and sort the things that happened to Alexander. The teams label their categories and team member #2 writes their categories on the chalkboard.

When one or more of the teams have come up with time-related system, point out how the story follows Alexander through his horrible day from morning to evening.

Explain that a narrative story usually depends on a time sequence, and that later in the lesson, they will need to use a time sequence to write about a story about a day when nothing seems to go right for them.

Teacher's Note: If none of the groups come up with time sequence, review the categories the teams used with the class and have each team resort their events trying to use a different system than before.

4 Sentence Combining using *Think-Pair-Share*

Explain to the students that when we write, we sometimes write in short sentences and sometimes we write in longer sentences. Using a variety of sentences captures the reader's interest.

Make a chart or a transparency from the **Sentence Combining** handout. Ask the students if they remember what type of sentences are used in *Alexander and the Terrible, Horrible, No Good, Very Bad Day*. Show the first group of sentences.

> **I went to sleep.**
> **I had gum in my mouth.**
> **I had gum in my hair**
> **I got out of bed this morning.**
> **I tripped on my skateboard.**
> **I dropped my sweater in the sink.**
> **The water was running.**

Ask the students to look at the sentences and find two that can be combined into one sentence. Students share them with a partner. The students look again to find another two sentences that can be combined and share them with a different partner.

Lesson 9

5 Sharing sentences using *RoundRobin* with Assigned Roles

Challenge the students to combine as many of the sentences as they can into one sentence and to write his or her sentence on a piece of paper.

Assign roles to the team members as follows:

#1 - **Reader**

#2 - **Checker:** to make sure all the information was included

#3 - **Task Master**

#4 - **Praiser**

Each team member writes his or her role on a piece of paper. Team member #1 reads his or her sentence and the others team members listen and respond according to their roles.

The role cards pass to the left and everyone has a new role. The new Reader reads his or her sentence and the others respond according to role. The process continues until everyone has had a chance to read.

6 Making a list of things that can go wrong using *Brainstorming*

Using small pieces of paper, each team brainstorms all the things that could happen to them on a horrible day.

7 Organizing the list of things that can happen on a horrible day using *Unstructured Sort*

Each team sorts their ideas in some way. The categories are labeled to help students in finding particular responses.

8 Practicing sentence combining using *Simultaneous RoundTable*

Explain that now the students will combine sentences using ideas for their stories. Each person selects a category from the sorting activity to use. All the categories should be covered, but if

 Teacher's Note: This process can be repeated with the other groups of sentences on the **Sentence Combining** handout.

necessary two people may use one category. Each person selects 3 or 4 ideas from the category and records them on a sheet of paper in short simple sentences. For example, if clothing was one of the categories:

My shirt is dirty.

My socks got all wet.

I couldn't find my shoes.

My favorite pants ripped.

Using Simultaneous RoundTable, the students pass around their short sentences for the others to combine. Each team member should try to combine the sentences in a different way.

9 Writing about a horrible day using *Independent Writing*

Using the ideas from the sentence combining (or starting over if a student wishes), students independently write a story about the day when nothing seemed to go right. Encourage them to use Alexander's refrain after each group of activities. They also can include where they would escape to (I think I'll go to

Lesson 9

Jeanne Stone: *Cooperative Learning & Language Arts: A Multi-Structural Approach*
Kagan Publishing • 1 (800) 933-2667 • www.KaganOnline.com   153

_____.) For the primary grade students, it may be helpful for them to write on **A Horrible Day** handout so they don't have to rewrite the refrain over and over again.

10 Responding to writing using *RoundRobin*

After students have completed their stories, they share their writings with their teams. Each person reads his or her story to the team two times. (Individual copies can be passed out to each person if the students or teacher have had copies made.) Team members listen so that they can point out the words and phrases that had an impact on them, summarize what they heard, or tell the writer how they felt when they were listening. Each student then, with a RoundRobin share around, comments on the writing. Examples of comments might be:

> **I liked the part when you said "…"**
>
> **I could tell your sister really bugged you because "…"**
>
> **The main point to me is …**
>
> **I felt _____ when you read the story.**

Extensions

A Wonderful Day
This lesson can be done having students write about a wonderful, fantastic, terrific, very good day.

Solutions
Students use 4-S Brainstorming to create ideas to help out those people that are having a day when nothing seems to go right. These ideas can be used for a class sort. After the ideas are sorted and labeled, each team takes one of the categories and, using Simple Projects, creates two or three idea pages that will be part of a class book — *If You're Having a Bad Day, You Have to Read This Book!*

Lesson 9

A Horrible Day

Write a story about what might happen to you on a horrible day.

_____

_____

_____

I could tell it was going to be a terrible, horrible, no good, very bad day.

_____

_____

_____

I knew it was going to be a terrible, horrible, no good, very bad day.
I think I'll move to _____ .

_____

_____

_____

It was a terrible, horrible, no good, very bad day.

_____

_____

_____

It was a terrible, horrible, no good, very bad day.
I think I'll move to _____ .

Lesson 9

Jeanne Stone: _Cooperative Learning & Language Arts: A Multi-Structural Approach_
Kagan Publishing • 1 (800) 933-2667 • www.KaganOnline.com

Sentence Combining

I went to sleep
I had gum in my mouth.
I had gum in my hair.
I got out of bed this morning.
I tripped on my skateboard.
I dropped my sweater in the sink.
The water was running.

_____

_____

_____

We went downstairs.
The elevator door closed.
My foot was in it.
We waited for my mom
She went to go get the car.
Anthony made me fall in the mud.
I started crying.
Nick said I was a crybaby.

_____

_____

_____

My bath was too hot.
I got soap in my eyes.
My marble went down the drain.
I had to wear my railroad-train pajamas.

_____

_____

_____

_____

Adapted from: *Alexander and the Terrible, Horrible, No Good, Very Bad Day* by Judith Viorst

Fairy Tale Express

Grades 3 - 8

Lesson-At-A-Glance

Domain:
Imaginative/Narrative

Academic Skill:
Listening: Listen in order to respond to another person's story
Speaking: Participate in a group discussion
Reading: Recall details about a story
Writing: Write an imaginative story

Structures:
- *Similarity Groups*
- *Mix-Freeze-Pair*
- *RoundRobin*
- *Brainstorming*
- *Unstructured Sort*
- *Team Discussion*
- *Team Tour*
- *Numbered Heads Together*
- *Team Word-Webbing*
- *Independent Writing*
- *Group Discussion*

Materials:
- At least one fairy tale or folk tale per group
- Fairy Tales handout
  - 1 card per student. If possible, they should match the fairy tales or folk tales the students will be using.
- 1 3x5 pad of paper and tape or Post-it notes per group
- 2 sheets chart paper per group
- Markers

Time:
2-3 language arts periods

Lesson Overview
Fairy tales have always had a place in students' lives. This lesson allows students to explore a variety of fairy tales and find characteristics common across them. These characteristics will then be incorporated into a student's own fairy tale.

Lesson Sequence
1 **Grouping by favorite stories using *Similarity Groups***

> **Teacher's Note:** Students should be familiar with the fairy tales or folk tales being used before starting this lesson.

Students think of their favorite fairy tale or folk tale and write the name of it on a small piece of paper. The students meet with others who share the same favorite fairy tale or folk tale. Within the similarity groups, the students pair and tell each other what their favorite part of the tale is. The students discuss what the important elements are in that tale. Have students share across the classroom what their favorite tale is and what its important elements are.

2 Random team formation using *Mix-Freeze-Pair*

Pass out the fairy tale or folk tale title-cards from the handout. Students mix among themselves, freezing at the teacher's direction. After pairing up with the person closest to them, the students share something they know about the tale on the card they are holding. They then trade cards. Students Mix-Freeze-Pair two or three more times, repeating the process.

The four students who have the same fairy tale title card form a team and sit down together.

3 Reading a folk or fairy tale using *RoundRobin or Paired Reading*

Give each team a copy of the folk or fairy tale named on their card. To review the tale they have, students pass the tale around the table, each reading a paragraph (or page) aloud.

-or-

The students can review the story by telling, in turn, about the picture found on each page.

-or-

If each group has two copies of their story, they can do Paired Reading. Working in pairs, the students read alternate paragraphs to each other.

4 Remembering elements of a story using *4-S Brainstorming*

Teacher's Note: During 4-S Brainstorming, roles that correspond to the 4 S's can be assigned:

#1 - Speed Captain
#2 - Silly Idea Captain
#3 - Suspend Judgement Captain
#4 - Synergy Captain

With #1 as a Recorder, students brainstorm as many things as they can about the tale they read. Each item is written on a separate Post-it note or small piece of paper. For example, if the students had Goldilocks and the Three Bears they might write: house, woods, porridge, broken chair, three bears, three beds, etc.

5 Sorting elements of a story using *Unstructured Sort*

Assign roles to the team members:

#1 - **Recorder** to move and position the ideas
#2 - **Consensus Maker** to make sure the whole team agrees on the placement and labels,
#3 - **Encourager** to make sure every one is participating,
#4 - **Publisher** to make sure the chart is easy to read and mounted on the wall when completed.

Students sort the ideas from the brainstorming by moving them around on their tables. Any number of categories are allowed as long as the students can justify why the ideas go in that category. After sorting, the students mount, and label by category, the ideas on chart paper.

6 Talking about the categories using *Team Discussion*

Students discuss the rationale of how the categories are set up on their chart.

7 Viewing other teams category charts using *Team Tour*

The completed category charts are mounted around the classroom. Each chart has a sheet of paper attached to it for responses.

Lesson 10

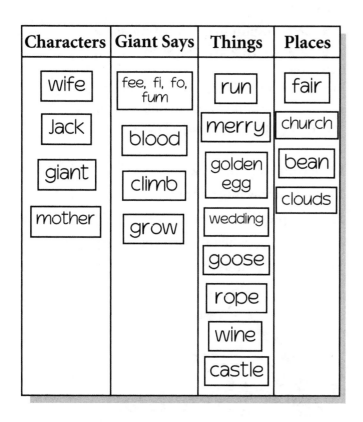

Characters	Giant Says	Things	Places
wife	fee, fi, fo, fum	run	fair
Jack	blood	merry	church
giant	climb	golden egg	bean
mother	grow	wedding	clouds
		goose	
		rope	
		wine	
		castle	

What happened at home	What happened in the forest	What happened at witch's house	What the people were	People
mother died	kids abandoned	witch died	poor	Mother
kids abandoned twice	kids lost	children eat house	blind witch	Father
took bread to make trail	kids follow trail	took jewelry	wood-cutter	Witch
took pebbles for trail	find food house	Gretel cooked	lonely dad	Gretel
		Gretel tricked the witch		Hansel

The teams select a Team Secretary that will record the team's comments on the comment sheets. Teams are encouraged to ask a question or make a comment about each chart they see.

Each team stands in front of their own chart. At the teacher's signal the teams pass to the next chart to review and respond to it. The teacher signals and they continue until they have viewed all the charts in the classroom.

8 Discussing the Gallery Tour comments using *Team Discussion*

Students return to their teams and discuss the questions and comments the other teams made about their own categories. The students also review the categories they noticed on the other charts.

9 Reviewing the categories using *Numbered Heads Together*

The teacher leads the class in summarizing the common characteristics that occurred in the fairy or folk tale charts. Quickly use Numbered Heads to find any commonalities in the tally. "Which category appeared the most? How many charts had identical categories?" Hopefully some of the students used a category with characters, setting, problem and solution.

10 Developing elements of a story using *Word-Webbing*

Remind the students that all imaginative stories have characters, a setting, a

Lesson 10

Jeanne Stone: *Cooperative Learning & Language Arts: A Multi-Structural Approach*
Kagan Publishing • 1 (800) 933-2667 • www.KaganOnline.com   159

problem, and a solution. Tell students that they will use these elements to create their own stories.

Using the following example, have students word-web ideas on a chart paper for creating a new imaginative tale. Each student has a different color marker and writes ideas for the different elements as he/she thinks of them. Have the group make any connections between ideas. See example.

11 Writing an Imaginative Tale using *Independent Writing*

Each student uses the different ideas from the word-web to write a new imaginative tale.

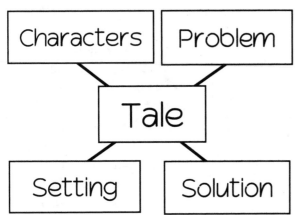

12 Responding to Writing using *Group Discussion*

Students read their completed imaginative tales to the team. Team members comment on their favorite part(s) of the story.

I like your story because _____.

I want to know more about _____.

I have a question about _____.

I felt _____when I heard your story.

Your story reminds me of _____.

Creating a New Tale
Students can change the elements in the word-web and create a new story. Using the categorizing from the fairy or folk tales, students can change just one of the elements and create a new story. For example, the three bears at the beach instead of in the woods.

Jeanne Stone: *Cooperative Learning & Language Arts: A Multi-Structural Approach*
Kagan Publishing • 1 (800) 933-2667 • www.KaganOnline.com

Fairy Tales

Prepare a title sheet with the eight folk tales you will be using. Duplicate it four times and cut it apart to use for the random card shuffle.

Lesson 10

Jeanne Stone: *Cooperative Learning & Language Arts: A Multi-Structural Approach*
Kagan Publishing • 1 (800) 933-2667 • www.KaganOnline.com

It Happened To Me One Day

Grades 3 - 8

Lesson-At-A-Glance

Domain:
Imaginative/Narrative

Academic Skill:
Listening: Listen to ask questions
Speaking: Relate a personal incident
Reading: Sequence events in chronological order
Writing: Write about an autobiographical incident

Structures:
- *Guided Imagery*
- *Fastwrite*
- *Three-Step Interview*
- *Independent Writing*
- *RoundRobin*

Materials:
- Samples of autobiographical writing (optional)
- Response Sheet handout

Time:
1-3 language arts periods

Lesson Overview

Most of us have events that we remember long after they really happen. Often the stories are retold again and again and become a part of the individual we are. This lesson gives students an opportunity to explore and record one such event in their lives.

This lesson will be strengthened if preceded by the opportunity for students to read or be read to from books containing autobiographical incidents. See Resource List for suggested readings.

Lesson Sequence

1 **Remembering a time before using** *Guided Imagery*

Teacher's Note: Guided Imagery texts are read slowly, giving students time to "see" their answers to the questions.

Guided Imagery

The teacher says, "Today you are going to write about a time in your life that is very memorable. Close your eyes. Take a deep breath. Think about a time in your life when you were very excited, very happy, or very sad. Close your eyes and imagine you are back at that same time and place. Remember this special time as I read the following questions. Where are you? What time is it? Is it winter or spring? Is it morning or evening? What day of the week is it? A weekend with a lot of people around? A school day? Look all around you. What do you see? What colors? What shapes? Listen carefully. What do you hear? Are there specific sounds or just a mesh of noises? Is it loud or quiet?

Guided Imagery (continued)

Can you smell anything? You're seeing the incident like it is on television. What happened first? Second? Next? How did you feel at the beginning? How did you feel at the end? Pretend you have a camera and take a picture of what you've seen and hold it in your mind. When I count to three, slowly open your eyes without losing the picture you have."

2 Recording ideas and images using *Fastwrite*

For ten minutes, have the students write as fast as they can without stopping. Have them record as many details as they can about the event they remembered.

3 Retelling the memory using *Three-Step Interview*

In pairs, students interview each other about the event they remembered and wrote about. During the interviews, the student includes the following three items.
1) The student tells the story.
2) The student tells why it's important to him or her.
3) The listening student asks a question such as:

> **Tell me more about _____.**
> **I don't understand_____.**
> **I liked the part when _____.**

In item three, the listener needs to ask questions to draw out more specific details.

After the interviews, the students RoundRobin to share a story they heard from each other.

4 Writing about a memory using *Independent Writing*

Students write about their events. They can use the fastwrite and elaborate on it or they can begin writing all over again. Students should be encouraged to tell the story using as many senses and feelings as they can.

5 Responding to writing using *RoundRobin*

After the students have completed their stories, have the students share their writings in their teams. Each person reads his or her story to the whole team two times. (Individual copies can be passed out to each student on the team if the student or teacher has had copies made.) Students listen so that they can point to the words and phrases that had an impact on them, summarize what they heard, and/or tell the writer how they felt when they were listening. Each student, using RoundRobin, comments on the writing. The comments can be recorded on the **Response Sheet** handout during the reading of the story.

Examples of comments might be:

> **I liked the part when you said "…"**
> **I could tell how important this was**
> **   to you because…**
> **The main point to me is …**
> **I felt _____ when you**
> **   read your story.**
> **I would like to know more about …**

Lesson 11

Resource List

Little House in the Big Woods by
Laura Ingalls Wilder

My Side of the Mountain by Jean George

Harriet the Spy by Louise Fitzhugh

Ben and Me by Robert Lawson

Boy: Tales of Childhood by Roald Dahl

Homesick: My Own Story by Jean Fritz

I, Juan de Pareja by Elizabeth Borton
de Trevino

*In the Year of the Boar and Jackie
Robinso*n by Bette Bao Lord

The War with Grandpa by
Robert Kimmel Smith

Lesson 11

Jeanne Stone: *Cooperative Learning & Language Arts: A Multi-Structural Approach*
Kagan Publishing • 1 (800) 933-2667 • www.KaganOnline.com

165

Response Sheet

What did you like best about this paper? What made it hold your attention?

_____

_____

_____

_____

What questions do you have? What is confusing or unclear to you?

_____

_____

_____

_____

What would you like to know more about? What needs more detail?

_____

_____

_____

_____

How would you rate this story on a scale of 1 (low) to 4 (high)? If you give a rating of 1 or 2, tell what you think would make the story better.

_____

_____

_____

_____

Lesson 11

Jeanne Stone: *Cooperative Learning & Language Arts: A Multi-Structural Approach*
Kagan Publishing • 1 (800) 933-2667 • www.KaganOnline.com

Fables

Grades 4 - 8

Lesson-At-A-Glance

Domain:
Imaginative/Narrative

Academic Skill:
Listening: Listen to storytelling
Speaking: Participate in a group discussion
Reading: Relate personal experiences to a fable
Writing: Write a new fable (Extension)

Structures:
- *Modeling*
- *Think-Pair-Share*
- *Partner Expert-Group Jigsaw*
- *Team Discussion*
- *Simple Project*
- *Team Interview*
- *Fastwrite*
- *RoundRobin*

Materials:
- Proverbs handout (Extension)
- Fable Outline handout (Extension)
- Compare/Contrast handout (Extension)
- "The Lion and the Mouse"
- "The Fox and the Crow"
- "The Crow and the Pitcher"
- "The Donkey Carrying Salt"
- Four fables - 1 per team (these or any other four)

Time:
2-3 language arts periods

Lesson Overview

This lesson explores the genre of fables, and like Arnold Lobel, ties them into a modern-day time frame. Students explore fables and their morals as originally written by Aesop and then match a favorite moral to a current day situation.

This lesson will be strengthened if preceded by students having an opportunity to read fables or have fables read to them.

Lesson Sequence

1 Telling a fable using *Modeling*

Introduce the lesson to the students by telling them that they will be learning about fables. Fables were said to have been first told by Aesop, a slave in sixth-century Greece. Fables are short stories that teach a moral. Usually animals are among the main characters.

Using "The Lion and the Mouse" or another common fable, tell (not read) the fable to the students.

2 Determining the moral using *Think-Pair-Share*

After listening to the fable, the students Think-Pair-Share about what the moral of the fable might be. After some class sharing, tell the students the moral in its original wording.

3 Learning a new fable using *Partner Expert-Group Jigsaw*

Pass out a set of four fables to each team; each set has the same fables. Each student selects a fable from the set. The class forms new groups based on the fables chosen. All students with the same fable form a new group. Within each of the new groups, each student finds a partner.

Working with a partner, the students read and learn the fable. If needed, they can take notes on the **Fable Outline** handout. They should be able to tell the basic story and the moral without referring to the Fable Outline.

Partners pair to make an expert group. Within the expert groups, the students review their fable, agree on its main points and the meaning of the moral of the fable.

The expert groups split into the two sets of original partners to practice telling each other their fable.

The students meet back with their teams. Each student tells his or her fable to the rest of the team. The students should allow for some discussion before stating the moral to allow the team to figure out what the moral is.

4 Choosing a fable to work with using *Team Discussion*

Each team discusses the relevancy of the fables just heard. They are to discuss which of the fables and morals is most pertinent to their lives and come to consensus on one they will continue work-

ing with. After coming to consensus, the team should write the moral of the fable in their own words.

5 Acting out a fable using *Modeling*

Using "The Lion and the Mouse" have a team volunteer to act the fable out. One of the team members can be the lion. One (or two) can be the mouse. The remaining one or two team members can be animals who pass by without helping, or animals that observe what is happening from a distance. Have the students act out the fable using the dialogue from the actual fable or paraphrasing it in their own words.

6 Acting out a fable using *Simple Project*

Each team reads the fable they selected. This can be Paired Reading or a reader can be selected from the team. The team then assigns roles (all team members must participate in some way) and improvises the action and dialogue in the fable.

Option: Have the teams present their fables to the class. Team Inside-Outside Circle can be used to share the fables with other teams.

7 Character role play using *Team Interview*

Starting with team member #2, a student, in the character role from the fable the team acted out, sits in the center of the team. The other team members ask questions relating to the fable and the character being portrayed. For example, in "The Lion and the Mouse" some sample questions for the mouse might be:

Lesson 12

Jeanne Stone: *Cooperative Learning & Language Arts: A Multi-Structural Approach*
Kagan Publishing • 1 (800) 933-2667 • www.KaganOnline.com

- How did you feel while you were chewing the lion's ropes?
- Did you really expect to be able to pay the lion back for his good deed?
- Were you afraid the lion might hurt you?

Some sample questions for the lion might be:

- Why do you think no other animals came to help you?
- Did you really think the mouse would be able to return the favor?

Repeat the process until all team members have been interviewed.

8 Personally relating to the fable using *Fastwrite*

Students write as fast as they can without stopping about how they personally relate to the fable and moral they have been working with. They could write about a personal incident that matches the moral, rewrite the moral in their own words, or write to explain the fable to a younger brother or sister.

9 Responding to writing using *RoundRobin*

Have the students RoundRobin to share their fastwrites (all or part).

10 Acting out a modern day fable using *Simple Projects*

Using the fastwrites as a starting point, each team discusses the moral with its application to today. Using one of the fastwrites or an idea that has developed during the discussion, each team creates a real-life situation that teaches the same moral. The real-life situation becomes a mini-play. Each team member must have

a role. Encourage the use of dialogue and action. When all the groups are ready, the mini-plays can be shared with the whole class.

Resource List

Aesop's Fables by Aesop (edited by Ann McGovern)
Three Aesop Fox Tales by Paul Galdone
Frederick's Fables by Leo Lionni
Fables by Arnold Lobel
Mousekin's Fables by Edna Mille

Extensions

Create a New Fable

The students have now become familiar with a number of fables and have created and acted out a new fable. The next step is to write a fable. Pass out a **Proverbs** handout to each student. Have them look over the handout and identify a proverb that could become a moral for their fable. Decisions that students must make before creating a fable can be recorded on the **Fable Outline** handout.

Compare/Contrast

Students (or teams) can select a current day fable (from Arnold Lobel or Leo Lionni) and compare it to one written by Aesop or LaFontaine. A Venn diagram may be helpful when doing this. See the **Compare/Contrast** handout.

Lesson 12

Proverbs

1. Do not begrudge to others what you cannot use yourself.
2. One trick deserves another.
3. Little friends may prove to be great friends.
4. Don't count your chickens before they hatch.
5. He who is too greedy may end up with nothing.
6. Don't try what is impossible.
7. Money has no true value if it is not used.
8. Be warned by what happens to others.
9. Think twice before you leap.
10. If you try to please all, you will please none.
11. A noble soul never forgets a kindness.
12. If you want something to be surely done, do it yourself.
13. Prepare today for the needs of tomorrow.
14. Slow and sure is better than fast and careless.
15. Borrowed feathers do not make fine birds.
16. It is a poor friend who deserts you when you are in trouble.
17. Kindness works better than force.
18. One good turn deserves another.
19. A liar will not be believed even when he tells the truth.
20. The wicked will always find an excuse for doing what they like.
21. Half a loaf is better than none.
22. He who is hard to please may get very little in the end.
23. Do unto others as you would have them do unto you.
24. A kingdom divided against itself can't stand.
25. Stretch your arm no further than your sleeve will reach.
26. Think before you act.
27. Never trust a flatterer.
28. Biggest is not always best.
29. Look before you leap.
30. Necessity is the mother of invention.
31. Slow and steady wins the race.
32. Don't pretend to be something that you are not.

Jeanne Stone: *Cooperative Learning & Language Arts: A Multi-Structural Approach*
Kagan Publishing • 1 (800) 933-2667 • www.KaganOnline.com

Fable Outline

Moral: _____

_____

_____

Characters: _____

_____

_____

Setting: _____

_____

_____

Problem: _____

_____

_____

Solution: _____

_____

_____

Lesson 12

Jeanne Stone: *Cooperative Learning & Language Arts: A Multi-Structural Approach*
Kagan Publishing • 1 (800) 933-2667 • www.KaganOnline.com   171

Fable Compare/Contrast

Jeanne Stone: *Cooperative Learning & Language Arts: A Multi-Structural Approach*
Kagan Publishing • 1 (800) 933-2667 • www.KaganOnline.com

All About Animals

Grades K - 2

Lesson-At-A-Glance

Domain:
Practical/Informative

Academic Skill:

Listening: Listen to order to paraphrase

Speaking: Tell about a favorite object
Paraphrase what was heard.

Reading: Classify animals by type (farm or wild), movement, & body covering

Writing: Dictate a report on how animals move, or on their body covering (Kindergarten)
Write a report on how animals move, or on body coverings (Grades 1, 2)

Structures:
- *RoundRobin*
- *Similarity Groups*
- *Think-Pair-Share*
- *Numbered Heads Together*
- *Team Project*
- *Partners*
- *Independent Writing*
- *Three-Step Interview*

Materials:
- 2 Animals Cards Set A handouts per team
- 2 Animals Cards Set B handouts per team
- 2 Animals Have Coverings handouts per team
- 2 Animals Move handouts per team
- Writing About Animals handout (optional)
- 1 6" x 6" white drawing paper per student
- Crayons, tape or glue, scissors (2 per team)
- Butcher paper (optional)

Time:
2-3 language arts periods

Lesson Overview

Animals are a common interest among children. Using this common interest, students share their favorite animals and create a class animal quilt. They will learn either how animals move or what their body coverings are and share it with their teammates.

Lesson Sequence

1 Listing animals using *RoundRobin*

The teacher introduces the lesson by asking students to think of as many different animals as they can that live on a farm. Students RoundRobin as many different farm animals as they can. Students think of as many different wild animals as they can and RoundRobin again.

Have team member # 2 pick up a white drawing paper for each team member. After thinking of a favorite animal, have each student draw and color his or her animal. Encourage them to make the picture large and fill the page so that the animal is easy to see.

2 Grouping by favorite animals using *Similarity Groups*

Taking their animal pictures with them, students find others in the class that like the same animal they do. Students with the same animal form similarity groups.

Encourage them to create groups of animal similarities if there are many one-person groups (a "cat" group, a "deer" group, etc.).

3 Talking about a favorite animal using *Think-Pair-Share*

In Similarity Groups, have the students Think-Pair-Share about:
1. **Why they like their animal.**
2. **What they don't like about their animal.**
3. **What would they do if they met their animal on the street.**

Have the students share across Similarity Groups.

4 Farm Animals vs. Wild Animals *Numbered Heads Together*

After students return to their teams, use Numbered Heads Together to reinforce the idea of farm animals versus wild animals. In Round 1, ask the teams to look at the animal picture being shown and be able to tell if it's a farm animal or a wild animal. In Round 2, name or describe an animal and ask if it is a farm animal or a wild animal. "Is a chicken a farm animal or a wild animal? Is a chimpanzee a farm animal or a wild animal?" In Round 3, select either a farm animal or wild animal and have the students be able to name an appropriate animal.

5 Animal mural using *Team Projects*

Each team needs to have pictures of two farm animals and two wild animals on the 6" by 6" white drawing paper. If the team does not have the right animals, they need to select an animal (animals) that they need and make pictures of them. While other pictures are being made, if necessary, have the other students RoundRobin and describe their animals.

When each team has the correct number and kind of animals, they are to tape them together as shown below:

As each team completes their "mini" mural, they are to mount it with the others to make a class mural. The final mural will be rectangular or square depending on the number of teams. With an odd number of teams, one team's section may need to be divided to make an even rectangle or square. The shape for eight teams would be four team murals across and two team murals down.

Team Mural	Team Mural	Team Mural	Team Mural
Team Mural	Team Mural	Team Mural	Team Mural

With seven teams, it would be three and a half team murals across across and two team murals down.

Lesson 13

Team Mural	Team Mural	Team Mural	1/2
Team Mural	Team Mural	Team Mural	1/2

With nine, it would be three team murals by three team murals.

Team Mural	Team Mural	Team Mural
Team Mural	Team Mural	Team Mural
Team Mural	Team Mural	Team Mural

6 Learning about animals using Partners

Explain to the class that they will now be working with partners to learn something new about animals and to teach it to their teammates. Divide each team into A Partners and B Partners. Give the A Partners an **Animal Cards-Set A** handout and a **How Animals Move** handout and two pairs of scissors. Give the B Partners one Animal Cards-Set A handout, a **Body Coverings** handout, and two pairs of scissors. Review the Animal Cards-Set A handout to make sure all students can identify the animals pictured on the cards.

Have the A partners go to one side of the room to work and the B partners to the other side. First, have the partners cut the animal pictures apart. After a brief discussion, the partners work together to sort and classify the animal cards

onto their sorting handout. When the sorting is completed by the A partners, they share their sorting sheet with other A partners to compare answers. When the sorting is completed by the B partners, they check their answers with other B partners.

At this point, model for the students an acceptable way for tutoring their teammates. For example, select a different topic such as "Where Animals Live" (in the water, on the ground, or in the trees). Here are possible steps you might use:

1. **Explain the topic.**
2. **Place two or three animal cards on the mat.**
3. **Ask the tutee to place the other animal cards, acting as a coach and checker.**

The partners return to their original teams. The A partners show their teammates how to sort the animal cards by how animals move. When the task is completed, the B partners show their teammates how to sort the cards by body coverings.

To check for understanding, distribute an **Animal Cards-Set B** handout to each team. Have the teams cut their animal cards apart. The teams then work together to sort how the animals move. When they are done and the teacher has monitored for correctness, the students glue the animals on the handout. Pass out another Animal Cards-Set B handout to each team. After cutting the animal cards apart, they sort the animals on the Body Coverings handout. After being checked for correctness, they can also be glued.

Lesson 13

7. Writing to summarize a chart using *Dictated Writing* (Kindergarten)

Each student selects one of the sorts the team has completed (How Animals Move or Body Coverings). Each student dictates one or two sentences about the chart. They can illustrate the sentences after they have read them back to the teacher.

8. Writing about animals using *Independent Writing* (Grades 1 and 2)

Students can write a report on animals' body coverings or how animals move. Each student selects one of the topics and summarizes what he or she sees on the appropriate chart. Each report should include an introductory statement such as: "Animals live in different places." or "Animals have different body coverings." Sample writing forms are included on the **Writing About Animals** handout.

9. Responding to writing using *Three-Step Interview*

Working in interview pairs, a student reads his or her writing to a partner. The partner summarizes what he or she heard and asks any questions. During RoundRobin, the students summarize the writing that their partner read.

After the Three-Step-Interview is completed, allow time for students to make any changes they wish. Comments and/ or questions from team members may encourage them to make changes to improve their writing.

3-Part Venn Diagram
Use the information the students learn to create a 3-part Venn diagram.
For example:

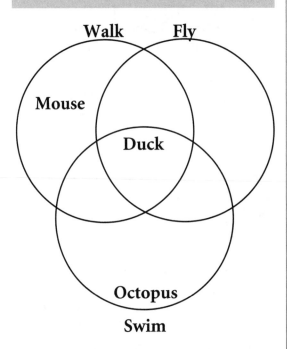

Lesson 13

Animal Cards

chimpanzee

snake

lizard

hummingbird

angel fish

zebra

turkey

lion

catfish

pigeon

eagle

camel

Lesson 13

Jeanne Stone: *Cooperative Learning & Language Arts: A Multi-Structural Approach*
Kagan Publishing • 1 (800) 933-2667 • www.KaganOnline.com

177

Animal Cards

salmon	ostrich	whale
mouse	bear	duck
toucan	bat	fly
tiger	octopus	parakeet

Jeanne Stone: *Cooperative Learning & Language Arts: A Multi-Structural Approach*
Kagan Publishing • 1 (800) 933-2667 • www.KaganOnline.com

Writing About Animals

How Animals Move

Animals move in different ways. _____ and

_____ swim in the sea. _____

and _____ walk or crawl on the land. _____

_____ and _____ fly in the air.

My favorite animal is the _____. It moves _____

_____.

Body Coverings

Animals have many different coverings. _____ and

_____ have fur. _____

and _____ have scales. _____

and _____ have feathers. _____

and _____ have smooth skin. My favorite animal

is the _____.

It is covered with _____.

Jeanne Stone: *Cooperative Learning & Language Arts: A Multi-Structural Approach*
Kagan Publishing • 1 (800) 933-2667 • www.KaganOnline.com

Animals Have Coverings

Fur	Feathers	Scaly Skin/Scales

Lesson 13

Jeanne Stone: *Cooperative Learning & Language Arts: A Multi-Structural Approach*
Kagan Publishing • 1 (800) 933-2667 • www.KaganOnline.com

Animals Move

Crawl or Walk   **Swim**   **Fly**

Jeanne Stone: *Cooperative Learning & Language Arts: A Multi-Structural Approach*
Kagan Publishing • 1 (800) 933-2667 • www.KaganOnline.com

Dear Tooth Fairy

Grades 1 - 3

Lesson-At-A-Glance

Domain:
Practical/Informative

Academic Skill:
Listening: Listen to others share
Speaking: Participate in group discussions
Reading: Relate personal experiences
Writing: Use correct, simple letter format

Structures:
- *Line-Ups*
- *Team Discussion*
- *RallyTable*
- *Numbered Heads Together*
- *Independent Writing*
- *Three-Step Interview*
- *Partner Editing*

Materials:
- Letters to the Tooth Fairy handout
- Dear Tooth Fairy handout

Time:
1-2 language arts periods

Lesson Overview

Loose teeth and the tooth fairy are very common experiences for school-aged children. This lesson catches this interest and uses it to help students learn the purpose and form for writing a simple letter.

Lesson Sequence

1 **Counting the number of teeth lost using *Line-Ups***

The teacher says, "Run your tongue along your teeth. Have you lost any teeth yet? Count how many baby teeth you have lost. Form a line that shows how many teeth you have lost. From the least number of lost teeth on this side on the room to the most number of lost teeth on that side of the room." Students form a Line-Up.

Teacher's Note: To extend this lesson into math, have the students form a living bar graph. This can then be recorded on a class graph, "Number of Lost Teeth." For example:

How many teeth have you lost?

6			
5			
4			
3			
2			
1			
2 teeth	3 teeth	4 teeth	5 teeth

Students pair up with the person next to them and share how they lost one of their teeth. For those that might not have lost any teeth, have them discuss methods they have heard, for pulling out loose teeth, or good reasons for not having lost any teeth. Turning the other way, have the students share what they did with their tooth after it fell out. Again for those who haven't lost any teeth, have them discuss what they would do if they lost a tooth. Have the students return to their seats.

2 Talking about the Tooth Fairy using *Team Discussion*

Ask the students if they have ever heard of the Tooth Fairy. In their groups, have them discuss these questions:

- **Have you ever heard of the Tooth Fairy?**
- **Who is the Tooth Fairy?**
- **What is her job?**
- **What does she look like?**

If there are some teams who have no concept of the Tooth Fairy, use Teams Consult to share what was discussed between teams and to help the teams understand the concept of the Tooth Fairy.

3 Dialogue with the "Tooth Fairy" using *RallyTable*

The team members number off 1 to 4. Team members #1 and #2 become partners and team members #3 and #4 become partners. The partners sit next to each other. Team members #1 and the #3 are going to pretend to be the Tooth Fairy. Team members #2 and the #4 will pretend to be a child who has lost a tooth. Beginning with team members #2 and #4, each set of partners is going to write a dialogue between a child and the Tooth Fairy. The "child" (team members #2 and #4) thinks of what he or she might say to the Tooth Fairy, writes it on a paper, and passes the paper to the Tooth Fairy (team members #1 and #3).

The "Tooth Fairy" reads what was written, writes a response, and passes it back to the "child." The process continues for eight to ten minutes (or longer if the students become involved in their roles). Allow enough time for at least two written interactions from each student.

4 Reviewing letter format using *Numbered Heads Together*

Say to the students, "Earlier you pretended to be talking with the Tooth Fairy. Another way to talk to someone is through a letter. Today we will write a letter to the Tooth Fairy."

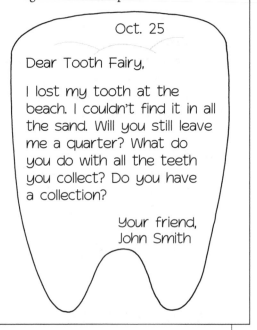

Teacher's Note: A letter written on a large tooth shape can serve as a model. The students can refer to the model when answering the questions in Numbered Heads Together. For example:

Oct. 25

Dear Tooth Fairy,

I lost my tooth at the beach. I couldn't find it in all the sand. Will you still leave me a quarter? What do you do with all the teeth you collect? Do you have a collection?

Your friend,
John Smith

Using Numbered Heads Together review the parts of a friendly letter with questions such as:

- **What is the first thing you write in a letter?** (the date)

Lesson 14

Jeanne Stone: *Cooperative Learning & Language Arts: A Multi-Structural Approach*
Kagan Publishing • 1 (800) 933-2667 • www.KaganOnline.com
184

- **How do you know who the letter is for?** (the greeting)
- **Name two ways you can close the letter.** (Your friend, Love, Yours truly, From)
- **What comes after the closing of the letter?** (your name)

5 Talking about what goes in the letter using *Team Discussion*

Have the students read the letters on the **Letters to the Tooth Fairy** handout. In their teams, have them discuss what kinds of things they would want to say in a letter to the Tooth Fairy.

6 Writing a letter to the Tooth Fairy using *Independent Writing*

Students write a letter to the Tooth Fairy.

7 Responding to writing using *Three-Step Interview*

Have the students share their letters during Three-Step Interview. After hearing the letter, have the listener pretend he or she is the Tooth Fairy and respond as if he or she had just gotten the letter in the mail. During RoundRobin, have each student share his or her favorite part of the letter he or she heard.

8 Editing writing using *Partner Editing*

When the students complete their letters, have them work with their partners and check for the proper letter mechanics. Looking at their partners' papers, the students check for:
- **Date** (with comma)
- **Greeting** (followed by a comma)
- **Body**
- **Closing** (followed by a comma)
- **Name**

Resource List

Little Rabbit's Loose Tooth by Lucy Bate
Arthur's Tooth by Marc Brown
Wobbly Tooth by Nancy Cooney
Tooth Fairy by Delores Dixon
Alligator's Toothache by
    Marguerite Dorian
Crocus by Roger Duvoisin
Tooth Fairy by Anita Feagles
Tooth for the Tooth Fairy by
    Louise Gunther
The Tooth Witch by Karlin, Nurit
The Tooth Book by Theodore Le Sieg
The Bear's Toothache by David McPhail
Doctor De Soto by William Steig
Tooth Fairy by Audrey Wood

Extensions

Dear Child
Have the students select a finished letter and respond to it as if they were the tooth fairy. Publish the letters and their responses in a book or on a bulletin board.

How to Remove a Loose Tooth
Write the step-by-step directions for removing a loose tooth. This could be done with a Simultaneous RoundTable. Each person would write a first step and as the papers pass around the team another step would be added.

Lesson 14

Letters to the Tooth Fairy

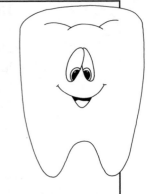

Dear Tooth Fairy,

I lost my tooth in my bed. I'm sorry but I can't give you my tooth, but please give me some money anyway.

> From,
> Rachel

Dear Tooth Fairy,

My brother and I need money for my Mom's birthday. Does it count if I knock out some of his teeth and we split the money?

> Mike
> P.S. My brother says it's okay.

Dear Tooth Fairy,

Here is my tooth. It is very valuable because it has silver in it. Please take care of it, and when you are all finished with it could I have it back?

> Thank you,
> Karen

Dear Tooth Fairy,

My Grandpa is visiting us and he has some teeth that he can take out whe ever he wants. Do you leave money for teeth if the teeth are not mine?
Just curious,

> Your friend,
> Danny

Dear Tooth Fairy,

My tooth is loose and I'm leaving for camp tomorrow. If it comes out at camp, do you deliver anywhere?

> Scott

Jeanne Stone: *Cooperative Learning & Language Arts: A Multi-Structural Approach*
Kagan Publishing • 1 (800) 933-2667 • www.KaganOnline.com

Dear Tooth Fairy...

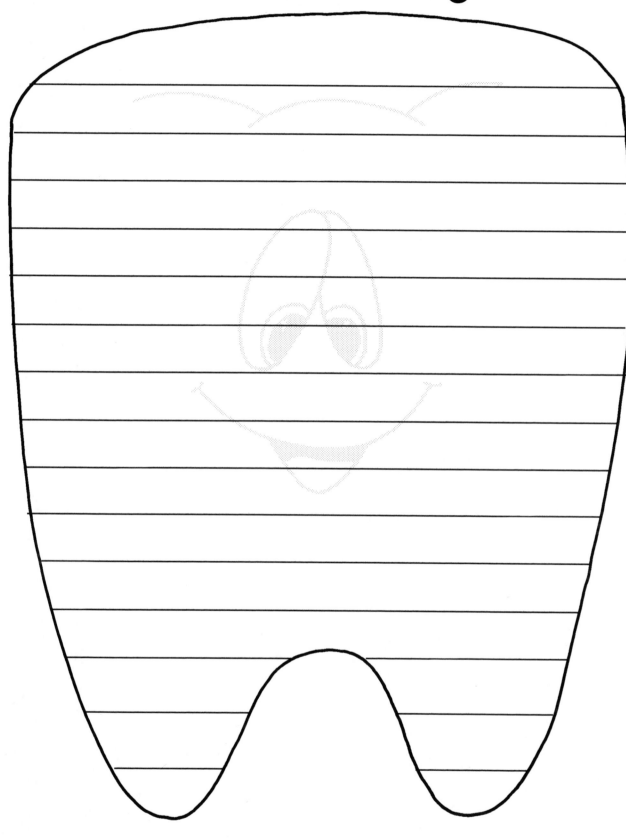

Jeanne Stone: *Cooperative Learning & Language Arts: A Multi-Structural Approach*
Kagan Publishing • 1 (800) 933-2667 • www.KaganOnline.com

Lesson 15

Who Are You?
An Interview

Grades 1 - 4

Lesson-At-A-Glance

Domain:
Practical/Informative

Academic Skill:
Listening: Listen to remember information
Speaking: Interview a peer or an adult
Writing: Record (or remember) information
Write (or dictate) an interview

Structures:
• *Teacher Talk*
• *Team Discussion*
• *Numbered Heads Together*
• *Class Brainstorming*
• *Modeling*
• *Three-Step Interview*
• *Independent Writing*
• *RoundRobin*

Materials:
• Sample interviews from magazines and newspapers (optional)
• Chart paper - 3 pieces
• Chart paper strips - 18 to 20
• A classroom visitor for modeling an interview

Time:
2-3 language arts periods

Lesson Overview

Playing on students' natural curiosity to know everything about what's going on around them, this lesson allows students to practice interviewing each other. After a practice interview and a chance to formulate interview questions, students go out into the world to interview someone they would like to know more about. The interview is then written up and shared with other members of the class.

Lesson Sequence

1 **Introducing Who Are You? An Interview using *Teacher Talk***

Tell the students that one way to learn about others and what they do is to interview them and that they are going to interview someone who is interesting to them. Share some examples of people they could interview: friends, school staff members (teachers, office staff, custodians), older students, community help-

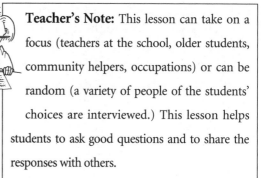

Teacher's Note: This lesson can take on a focus (teachers at the school, older students, community helpers, occupations) or can be random (a variety of people of the students' choices are interviewed.) This lesson helps students to ask good questions and to share the responses with others.

Jeanne Stone: *Cooperative Learning & Language Arts: A Multi-Structural Approach*
Kagan Publishing • 1 (800) 933-2667 • www.KaganOnline.com   **189**

ers, public figures, or parents. Have the students on each team number off 1, 2, 3, and 4.

Optional: If you have collected sample interviews from newspapers and magazines, they can be shared with the class now.

2 Learning about interviews using *Team Discussion*

Ask the students what an "interview" is and have them discuss it in their teams. With team member #3 as the reporter, the teams share their answers. On a piece of chart paper, synthesize the teams' responses and write a definition for "interview." Post it so that the class can see it and can refer back to it throughout the lesson.

Repeat the above steps with the terms "reporter" and "question." Use team member #2 as the reporter for "reporter" and team member #4 as the reporter for "question."

3 Reviewing statements and questions using *Numbered Heads Together*

Round One: Read a series of statements and questions to the students. The teams put their heads together and decide if it is a question or a statement. Call a number for a response. The students can respond together with thumbs up for questions or thumbs down for statements. Some sample statements and questions are:

> What is your favorite thing to do?
> I like to ride my bike.
> Roses are my favorite flowers.
> Who is your favorite person and why?

> Did you always want to be a teacher (policeman, fireman)?
> I like to listen to sirens and watch fire trucks race by.

Round Two: Students put their heads together and think of some questions on their own. Call a number for students to respond.

Teacher's Note: Instead of thumbs up and thumbs down, response cards can be prepared showing a period on one side and a question mark on the other side. Students hold up the correct response card when the answer is called for.

Round Three: After hearing a variety of questions, students put their heads together and think of words that usually begin questions. When the students respond, put the words on a class <u>Question Words</u> chart.

Question Words
Who?
What?
When?
Where?
Why?
How?
Which?

4 Listing people to interview using *Class Brainstorming*

The students brainstorm people they would be interested in interviewing - people they would like to know more about. Call on #1's to give ideas and record their responses on a class chart — <u>People I'd Like to Know More About</u>. Continue with #2's, #3's and #4's giving each group of students a chance to respond. At the end open it up for responses from anyone. Review the chart with the students when it is completed.

Jeanne Stone: *Cooperative Learning & Language Arts: A Multi-Structural Approach*
Kagan Publishing • 1 (800) 933-2667 • www.KaganOnline.com

5 Creating interview questions using *Team Discussion*

The students discuss questions they might ask the person in an interview. When the team has two or three good questions they send a reporter to report to the teacher. The teacher records the questions on a <u>Class Question Chart</u> deleting any duplicate questions. Make sure all teams have had a chance to contribute at least one question to the list.

6 Viewing an actual interview using *Modeling*

With the question list prepared, the students are ready to see an actual interview. As the interviewer, select two or three questions (adjust the number according to the grade level) from the question list and decide what order they will be asked in. Have a visitor come to the classroom to be interviewed. (This person should fit the criteria for who can be interviewed if any was set earlier in the lesson.)

7 Writing up an actual interview using *Modeling*

When the interview is completed, have the class participate in writing up the interview. As the students suggest sentences to include in the written interview, record the sentences on strips of chart paper. After all the sentences are compiled, the students can begin reviewing the sentences to sequence them in a logical order. Using a pocket chart or tape, arrange the sentences in a logical order.

Teacher's Note: For additional practice, the peer interview can be written up *after* the RoundRobin.

8 Practicing an interview using *Three-Step Interview*

Using Three-Step Interview, the students interview their teammates. To prepare for the interview, each student must write three to five questions he or she will ask during the interview. Each question can be recorded on a separate sheet of paper to allow for notetaking (if desired). Each student also needs to decide in what order the questions will be asked.

The students interview their partners and then switch roles.

The students RoundRobin what they learned about the person they were interviewing.

9 Writing up an interview using *Independent Writing*

Each student selects a person to interview from the chart <u>People I'd Like to Know More About</u>. As a homework assignment, the student interviews the person he or she has selected. If the people being interviewed are school personnel, interview times can possibly be set up before or after school or at recess.

Students write up the interview.

10 Sharing the interview using *RoundRobin*

Students can share their written interviews in RoundRobin groups for response from the other students. After each student has read their interview, students RoundRobin around the team sharing a positive response and a question about something else they might

<u>*Lesson 15*</u>

want to know about the person who was interviewed. Peer response gambits can be written on a chart paper or chalkboard to be used during the RoundRobin. Some examples of gambits might be:

I liked the part when you said "..."
I could "see" a picture of the person you interviewed when you said...
I could tell how you felt about the person you interviewed because...
To me the main point of what you learned was...
I would like to know more about...

xtensions

Interview Book
The interviews in this lesson can be collated into a book for the class library. This lesson can be one in a series that uses focused interview topics to create books on different topics. For example:

What Do You Want to Be When You Grow Up?
Interviews with people from different occupations

Living in the Past
Interviews with people who lived at least 50 years ago

Where in the World Are You?
Interviews with people who have lived in different parts of the world.

Illustrated Interviews
A drawing can be made or a photograph taken of the person interviewed to be displayed along side the finished interview.

Dialogue
This lesson can be extended to the upper grades and have the interview reported in dialogue form.

Historical Figures
After intense study have students portray different historical figures from a particular time period. Have them be interviewed as that person.

Lesson 15

Jeanne Stone: *Cooperative Learning & Language Arts: A Multi-Structural Approach*
192   Kagan Publishing • 1 (800) 933-2667 • www.KaganOnline.com

Lists Galore

Grades 2 - 6

Lesson-At-A-Glance

Domain:
Practical/Informative

Academic Skill:
Listening: Listen to others share
Speaking: Participate in a team discussion
Reading: Classify ideas into categories
Writing: Write to chart information
Use a period after a number in a list
Capitalize the first word in each item on a list

Structures:
- *Think-Pair-Share*
- *Team Discussion*
- *Simultaneous RoundTable*
- *4S Brainstorming*
- *RoundTable*
- *Numbered Heads Together*
- *Team Projects*
- *Gallery Tour*

Materials:
- List handouts - 1 each of four different lists per team
- Grocery List chart
- Chart paper - 1 per team and 1 per class
- Small papers for Brainstorming
- Crayons or markers - 1 set per team
- "Sarah Cynthia Sylvia Stout Would Not Take the Garbage Out" by Shel Silverstein in *Where the Sidewalk Ends*

Time:
2 or 3 language arts periods

Lesson Overview

Not all writing students do is in essay form. This lesson is light-hearted instruction in making lists and creating charts. After practicing on a class list, each team will choose a topic to create their own team list.

Lesson Sequence

1 **Thinking of excuses using**
Think-Pair-Share

Read "Sarah Cynthia Sylvia Stout Would Not Take the Garbage Out" by Shel Silverstein to the class. Have the students think of reasons or excuses that Sarah would have for not taking the garbage out. After sharing them with a partner, have the students do a quick **Stand-Up and Share*** and record the reasons or excuses on a class chart labeled <u>Reasons for Not Taking the Garbage Out</u>.

***Stand-Up and Share:** All students stand up. Starting at one side of the room, students one by one give the answer that they have and sit down. If anyone else in the room is thinking of the same answer, they sit down also.

2 **Adding to a list using**
Team Discussion

Explain to the students that they just finished making a list of excuses. There are many other reasons to make lists. One of them is a grocery list. Post the <u>Grocery List</u> chart in front of the class.

Grocery List

1. Milk
2. Eggs
3. Cheese
4. Bread
5. Apples
6. Tomatoes
7. Rice
8. Pork & Beans
9. Hot Dogs
10. Dish Soap

The students review the grocery list and discuss in their teams something else that could be added to the list. Team member #3 is the reporter from each team to come up and add one or two items to the grocery list. Remind the recorders to check the list before adding their items to make sure there are no duplicates.

3 Making lists using *Simultaneous RoundTable*

Post the following list topics on a chart paper or on the chalkboard. Team member #4 picks up a piece of paper for each team member. Each student writes a different list topic (from those posted or their own idea) on the top of the paper. The students use Simultaneous RoundTable to record ideas on the different lists as they are passed around.

List Topics

- Reasons for going to the movies
- Things to do in a hurry
- Foods that begin with the letter "B"
- Birthday presents we'd like to get
- Excuses for not having my homework
- Things to pack for vacation
- Food to eat at a party
- Things you would say "NO" to
- Things you would say "YES" to

Options for Sharing:

- Use **Teams Consult** to have the teams share some of the ideas they had for the different lists.

- Have team member #3's record one or two of their favorite ideas on matching class lists mounted in the front of the classroom.

4 Listing topics for a team list using *4S Brainstorming*

Tell the students that they will now create their own team lists on whatever topic they choose. Students brainstorm all the different list topics they can think of.

5 Select a topic for a list using *Team Discussion*

Each team selects one of their list topics. This will be the topic for the list that team will make for the class list book.

Option: If students cannot come to consensus on a list topic, introduce **Spend-A-Buck**. Each student is given four imaginary quarters to spend on any of the topics, but not more than two quarters can be spent on any one topic. After each team member has spent their quarters, the amount is totaled. The topic with the highest dollar value is selected as the team's choice.

6 Listing items for the list using *RoundTable*

After the topics are selected, the teams RoundTable the items that could appear on their lists.

Teacher's Note: It will be more convenient if the students can record each idea on separate piece of paper to facilitate prioritizing them in the next part of the lesson.

Lesson 16

7 Reviewing the format of a list using *Numbered Heads Together*

Students refer to the class lists to answer questions about the format for a list. Use questions such as:

Where are the numbers lined up on the list? (on the left)

What punctuation is used after the number? (period)

What do you notice about the first word in every item on the list? (It's capitalized.)

What can you tell me about the title of the list? (It's centered and capitalized.)

Are the items written continuously? (No, each item is written on a new line.)

Teacher's Note: Before writing the list remind the students to use a dictionary, another team or the teacher to check the spelling of all items they are adding to the list. The final list should be drafted on paper and submitted for teacher monitoring before the list is created for presentation on chart paper.

8 Making a list using *Team Project*

Each team selects ten or twelve items from the RoundTable list to go on the presentation list.

The final presentation list will be made on chart paper and decorated in some way to go along with the theme of the list. Each student should select one color to use on the chart and all of the colors must be represented.

9 Viewing other teams' lists using *Gallery Tour*

Students prepare a sheet for comments and additions to the list. A piece of paper is folded in half vertically and the left column is labeled "Comments" and the right column is labeled "List Additions." The paper is attached to each team's list. All the lists are posted in the classroom. As teams tour around the room they can write a comment and add any additional ideas for the list on each team's sheet.

Extensions

Sorts
Have the students categorize the items they created during the RoundTable. How many different ways can they be reclassified? What other lists can be made?

Trade-A-Problem
Each team creates two or three list topics and eight or ten items for each list. Each of these is written on a separate piece of paper. They are all placed in an envelope and traded with another team. Each team sorts the items onto the appropriate lists. The teams check each other's sorts and put all the pieces back into the envelope and trade with another team.

Lesson 16

A Special Place

Grades 5 - 8

Lesson-At-A-Glance

Domain:
Practical/Informative

Academic Skill:
Listening: Listen to paraphrase
Speaking: Paraphrase what was said
Reading: Drawing conclusions from what was read
Writing: Write to give clear directions
Write to report on a particular place

Structures:
- *Line-Ups*
- *Guided Imagery*
- *Three-Step Interview*
- *Fastwrite*
- *Team Discussion*
- *One Stray*
- *Independent Writing*
- *RoundRobin*

Materials:
- Travel sections from newspapers and magazines
- A Special Place handouts

Time:
2 language arts periods

Lesson Overview

Just as Dorothy said in the movie Wizard of Oz, there is a place that everyone dreams of somewhere over the rainbow. This lesson has students remember that special place and share it with their teammates. They then write a travel report to encourage people to visit it.

> **Teacher's Note:** If you wish, ask students to bring a picture of them in their special place. They can use the picture to help focus before the Guided Imagery and during the Fastwrite.

Lesson Sequence

1 Sharing special places using *Line-Ups*

Tell the students to think of a special place they would like to go. This can be a place they enjoy because it is quiet and peaceful, or because it is full of people, noise, and excitement. Have them think of how long it takes to get to their special place. The students line-up by either the time or distance it takes them to travel to this special place. Starting on each end of the line-up, students turn to face a partner.

They discuss whether the distance they would have to travel to go to their special place makes it easy for them to go frequently or keeps them from going very often. Someone at each of the extremes (near and far) and in the middle of the line-up share their feelings about the distance from their special place with the class. After each share, students paraphrase what they heard with their partners.

2 Remembering a special place using *Guided Imagery*

Explain to the students that no matter how far their special place is, they can go there whenever they want to by using their memories. Tell the students that they will be going on a imaginary trip to their favorite place. Have them close their eyes, sit back, and relax. Read the following text slowly, allowing the students time to develop images of their special place.

Guided Imagery

Imagine yourself at home. You are getting ready to leave for your special place. As you travel there, look around you, where are you going? How are you traveling? What sights do you see that could act as landmarks for someone traveling there for the first time? Are there are special sounds you hear? Does the weather change as you are traveling, or does it remain the same? You are arriving at your special place. How much time has elapsed?

As you look around your special place make special note of all that you see. What do you see? What small details have been blended to make this a complete scene for you? Can you look at it as if you are seeing it for the first time? How do you feel? Is it warm or cold? What do you hear? What do you smell? What do you notice about the people around you? Are they active or still? Are you with many people or just a few?

Though you could probably stay at this special place much longer, begin the journey home. Again, look at the surroundings. Is there anything you missed the first time passing by?

When you arrive back home, take a deep breath and slowly open your eyes, trying to maintain a picture of this special place.

3 Sharing a special place using *Three-Step Interview*

Students share their special place in a Three-Step Interview. Encourage them to share in such a way that the person who is listening could give specific directions to a stranger about how to get there and what they would find once they got there. During Step 3, RoundRobin, the partner should listen as his or her special place is being described by the other partner. What elements or special characteristics were left out? What other information would have helped the partner? Take notes on the **A Special Place** handout.

4 Writing about the special place using *Fastwrite*

Students fastwrite for ten or fifteen minutes. They should concentrate on describing as much as they can about their special place including the directions on how to get there. Remind them to think back to the "trip" they took earlier, as well as look at the notes they took when someone else described their special place.

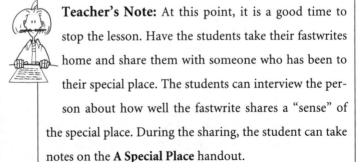

Teacher's Note: At this point, it is a good time to stop the lesson. Have the students take their fastwrites home and share them with someone who has been to their special place. The students can interview the person about how well the fastwrite shares a "sense" of the special place. During the sharing, the student can take notes on the **A Special Place** handout.

Lesson 17

5 Discussing common characteristics of travel reports using *Team Discussion*

The next day, have the students read some travel reports from newspapers and magazines. After reading one or two, have the students discuss in their teams, which reports were especially clear while they were reading. What made them feel as if they were traveling along? With team member #3 as the recorder, have them record sample parts of the text that helped make strong mental pictures and involved them in the trip. The teams should be ready to share their examples and tell why they selected it as an example.

6 Sharing examples using *One Stray*

One member from each team rotates through all the other teams, sharing the examples they selected from the travel reports. When the teams are finished sharing, have the teams discuss what commonalities they found during the One Stray and have team member #2 share with the class. Create a class list to show what creates strong pictures in writing (sensory details, similes, metaphors, personal anecdotes).

7 Writing a travel report using *Independent Writing*

Using the ideas gained from the travel reports and the ideas they generated during the interview and the fastwrite, students write a travel report on their special place. Remind them to include clear directions on how to get there and a description of what the special place is like.

8 Responding to writing using *Three-Step Interview*

Working in Interview pairs, students read their travel reports to each other.

Encourage the students to ask questions of each other when they are reading. During RoundRobin, the students summarize their partner's travel report. As the partners summarize what they heard, the student who described the special place may want to use the A Special Place handout to rate themselves on how clearly he or she pictured the special place and take notes for revising the writing later. After the Three-Step Interview is completed, allow time for students to make any changes they wish. Comments and/ or questions from team members may encourage them to make changes to improve their writing.

xtensions

A Special...
Have the students write a report on something that is special to them. Instead of a special place, have them choose one of the following:

A Special Person

A Special Hobby

A Special Pet

A Special Tool

A Special ...

Lesson 17

Jeanne Stone: *Cooperative Learning & Language Arts: A Multi-Structural Approach*
Kagan Publishing • 1 (800) 933-2667 • www.KaganOnline.com   199

A Special Place

Directions

Senses

Sight

Sound

Smell

People

Special Characteristics and Landmarks

Jeanne Stone: *Cooperative Learning & Language Arts: A Multi-Structural Approach*
Kagan Publishing • 1 (800) 933-2667 • www.KaganOnline.com

A Special Place

As you listen to a partner summarize your writing, rate how well you communicated the following ideas about your special place. Make notes on what you might want to change to improve your writing.

Directions

Clear   Not Clear
10   1

Senses

Created Images   Does Not Create Images
10   1

     Sight

     Sound

     Smell

People

Real-life descriptions   Not mentioned
10   1

Special Characteristics and Landmarks

Picture-like   Not Picture-like
10   1

Lesson 17

Sounds Around

Grades K - 2

Lesson-At-A-Glance

Domain:
Sensory/Descriptive
Analytical/Expository

Academic Skill:
Listening: Identify sounds students hear
Sort sounds into loud & soft
Rate sounds as louder or softer
Speaking: Participate in group discussion
Reading: Relate personal experiences to the story
Classify objects
Writing: Complete sentences

Structures:
• *RoundRobin*
• *Teacher Talk*
• *Think-Pair-Share*
• *4S Brainstorming*
• *Structured Sort*
• *Team Discussion*
• *Independent Writing*

Materials:
• 1 I Can Hear handout or Louder and Softer handout per student
• Books about sound (see Resource List)
• Covered boxes or cans with items that make sound (optional)
• Tape recording with various sounds on it (optional)
• Small pieces of paper
• 1 large 12" x 18" construction paper per team

Time:
1 language arts period

Lesson Overview
Every day life is full of sounds. This lesson leads students in exploring sounds and rating these sounds as loud or soft. Students summarize their learning with a writing (or dictating) activity.

This lesson can easily be adapted to work with the other senses. See the Resource List for books and poems pertaining to the other senses.

Lesson Sequence

1 Listing sounds heard using *RoundRobin*

Tell the students to sit very quietly in the classroom and listen to all the sounds they hear around them. (You might want to make sure the classroom door is open so students can hears sounds inside and out.)

After about two minutes, students RoundRobin all the different sounds they heard. Encourage them to make the sound and tell what made the sound.

2 Discovering sounds using *Teacher Talk* or *Think-Pair-Share*
There are a variety of ways to further introduce sound to the students.

Option #1 with *Teacher Talk*

Select two or three books about sound and read them to the students. Have them imitate some of the sounds in the book and review the things that they can think of that make noise.

Option #2 with *Think-Pair-Share*

Prepare four or five sound containers (sealed containers with different objects inside). Shake the containers one at a time. Use Think-Pair-Share for students to guess what object might be making the noise. After the class share, show the students the object that made the sound. Continue until all of the sound containers have been shared. Some ideas for sound containers are:

coins	marbles
rocks	marshmallows
a bell	sand
crinkled paper	popcorn kernels

Option #3 with *Think-Pair-Share*

Prepare a tape recording of different sounds. Play the sounds one at a time and the students Think-Pair-Share what they think the sound might be. Some ideas for the taped sounds are:

car engine	telephone ringing
door slamming	whistle blowing
ball bouncing	paper tearing
hands clapping	siren

3 Listing sounds using *4S Brainstorming*

Students brainstorm different things that make sounds. These can be recorded by drawing or writing each thing on a separate, small piece of paper. As the teacher monitors the brainstorming, ask the students to clarify any confusing pictures and label them.

4 Sorting loud and soft sounds using *Structured Sort*

Students review the items they brainstormed. They sort them into <u>Soft Sounds</u> and <u>Loud Sounds</u>.

> **Teacher's Note:** Prepare the sorting sheets for the students. Fold a large 12" x 18" piece of construction paper in half the long way. Holding the paper vertically, label one column Soft Sounds and the other Loud Sounds.

Soft Sounds	Loud Sounds
Rain	Thunder
Footstep	Drum
Whisper	Bell
Music	Dog barking
Ocean Waves	Yelling

5 Discussing the Sound Chart using *Team Discussion* with *Talking Chips*

Using Talking Chips, have the teams discuss what they see on their chart. As each team member makes a comment, he or

Lesson 18

she places his or her pencil in the center of the table. When all the team's pencils are in the center, each student collects his or her own pencil and the process starts again. Encourage comments such as:

Something I can hear is...

Something I can not hear is...

A _____ makes a loud sound.

A _____ makes a soft sound.

A _____ is louder than a _____.

A _____ is softer than a _____.

6 Writing about sounds using *Independent Writing*

Share the writing frames handouts **I Can Hear** or **Louder and Softer** with the students. Allow them to select the frame they wish to complete. Kindergarten students may dictate the words they wish to use to complete the patterns or may complete the patterns with pictures.

Extensions

Sound Tapes
As a team project, have the students brainstorm a list of sounds they could put on a sound tape. With help at home or at school, have the students make a sound tape that other students can use to identify the sounds they hear.

Unless...
Extend the comparing pattern to **A _____ is louder than a _____ unless...**

For example: A typewriter is louder than a telephone unless the telephone is ringing.

Loudest and Softest
Use the following pattern sentences with the students:

_____ is loudest when _____.

_____ is softest when _____.

For example: A baby is loudest when it is crying.

A young boy is quietest when he is sleeping.

Sound Effect Stories
Listening to a group of sounds on a tape, students list what make the sounds and incorporate those sounds into a story in the order they were heard on the tape. A perfect place to start is to use Disney's "Sounds of a Haunted House" at Halloween time.

Lesson 18

Resource List

Books about Sound

Gobble, Growl, and Grunt by Peter Spier
Crash, Bang, Boom by Peter Spier
Plink, Plink, Plink by Byrd Baylor
Bam, Zam, Zoom by Ee Merriam
Hearing by Maria Ruis
Listen to the Rain by Bill Martin, Jr.
Sounds of a Summer Night by May
Garelick
The Listening Walk by Paul Showers
Sounds of Sunshine, Sounds of Rain by
Florence P. Heide
The Noisy Book series by Margaret Wise
Brown
Do You Hear What I Hear? by Helen
Borten
Listen to My Seashell by Charlotte Steiner
What's That Noise? by Lois Kaufman

Poem about Sound

"Ears Hear" by Lucia and James L.
Hymes, Jr.*

Books about Taste

Growing Vegetable Soup by Lois Ehlert
Pancakes for Breakfast by Tomie de Paola
Bread and Jam for Francis by Russell
Hoban
Blueberries for Sal by Robert McCloskey
Green Eggs and Ham by Dr. Seuss
The Popcorn Book by Tomie de Paola
Taste by Maria Ruis
What's That Taste by Kate Petty and Lisa
Kopper
Think About Tasting by Henry Pluckrose

Poems about Taste

"The Meal" by Karla Kuskin*
"Crunck and Lick" by Dorothy Aldis*
"Yellow Butter" by Mary Ann
Hoberman*
"Mix a Pancake" by Christina Rossetti*

* in *Read Aloud Rhymes for the Very Young*
selected by Jack Prelutsky

Lesson 18

Jeanne Stone: *Cooperative Learning & Language Arts: A Multi-Structural Approach*
Kagan Publishing • 1 (800) 933-2667 • www.KaganOnline.com
206

I Can Hear...

I can hear a _____.

I can hear a _____.

I can hear a _____.

I cannot hear a _____.

Lesson 18

Name _____

 # Louder and Softer

A _____ is louder than a

_____.

A _____ is louder than a

_____.

A _____ is softer than a

_____.

A _____ is softer than a

_____.

Dinosaurs

Grades 2 - 4

Lesson-At-A-Glance

Domain:
Analytical/Expository

Academic Skill:
Listening: Listen to learn information
Speaking: Paraphrase what was said
Reading: Recall information about dinosaurs
Writing: Write to compare and contrast meat-eating and plant-eating dinosaurs

Structures:
- *Corners*
- *RoundTable*
- *Partners*
- *Modeling*
- *Team Project*
- *Independent Writing*
- *Three-Step Interview*
- *Simultaneous RoundTable*

Materials:
- Dinosaur handouts for Corners
- Blank class chart labeled Dinosaur Facts
- Books or readings about dinosaurs-could be separate library books, science books, or copies of articles - or -
- 1 Meat-eating Dinosaurs and Plant-eating Dinosaurs handout per team
- 2 Dinosaur Note-taking handouts per team
- Strip Book Handout - teacher directions
- 2 Strip books per team - 8 to 10 3" x 24" strips of paper folded in half and stapled on fold to make 3" x 12" book
- 1 pair scissors per group
- 1 red and green marker per group

Time:
1-2 language arts periods

Lesson Overview
Dinosaurs are a high interest topic for children of all ages. This lesson explores the differences between meat-eating and plant-eating dinosaurs. Working in pairs, the students will learn about either meat-eating or plant-eating dinosaurs and then teach their teammates. The students will also learn a way to organize information before writing.

Lesson Sequence

1 Choosing a dinosaur using *Corners*

Ask the students how many of them are familiar with dinosaurs. Have them think about the dinosaurs they know. Mount the dinosaur signs: Bronto-saurus, Tyrannosaurus Rex, Stegosaurus, and Ornithomimus in the four corners of the room. Tell the students to think about these four common dinosaurs. Students pick one, write its name on a small piece of paper, and then go to the appropriate corner (near the matching dinosaur sign). Within the corners, students pair and share everything they know about the dinosaur they chose. The pairs pair and RoundRobin. A student from one of the corners shares what he or she learned during the Round-robin. Then a student in one of the other groups paraphrases what was said. Continue until all the corners share the information they discussed.

Option: Rather than paraphrasing across corners, the students paraphrase with a partner what was shared.

2 Listing facts about dinosaurs using *RoundTable*

After returning to their seats, each team RoundTables as many facts as they can about dinosaurs. These can be facts they heard during Corners or facts they already knew. Each team picks two or three facts to record on the class chart <u>Dinosaur Facts</u>. The recorder, team member #1, writes these on a piece of paper and then records them on the class chart. Remind the students to only record new ideas. (Before recording the facts on the chart, the teacher may want to check the recorder's notes for accuracy and spelling.)

Tell students that they already have some information about dinosaurs and they will be learning more about dinosaurs in the following Partners activity.

3 Learning about dinosaurs using *Partners*

Within the teams, form partners A and partners B (two students who will work together on the same material). Have the A partners all sit on one side of the classroom and the B partners all sit on the other side of the classroom. Distribute the materials (books, articles, stories) or the **Meat-eating Dinosaurs** and **Plant-eating Dinosaurs** handouts and the **Dinosaur Note-taking** handout.

Working in partners, the students master the materials. Partners A will study plant-eating dinosaurs and partners B will study meat-eating dinosaurs. They read the materials provided and record the information on the **Dinosaur Note-taking** handout. The A partners pair up with each other to make groups of four. The B partners do the same. The new groups of four compare information, checking for accuracy and additional information that may not have been available in the sources they were using. The partners organize the information so it can be quickly presented to their teammates.

The teams reunite and share the information they have learned. The A partners tell about plant-eating dinosaurs and the B partners tell about meat-eating dinosaurs. This is done orally.

4 Teaching how to make Strip Books using *Modeling*

Stop the groups at this point so the teacher can provide the information on how the students will organize the information they have. Tell the students that they will be learning a way to record and organize information. Using a large strip book, record "All dinosaurs..." on the front page. Have the students complete the sentence "All dinosaurs..."

> **All dinosaurs...**
> **...lived a long time ago.**
> **...lived in or near a swamp.**
> **...were different sizes.**

Record each response on a different page in the strip book. Stop periodically to reread all the sentences that have been written so far. Each time rereading the opening phrase.

> **All dinosaurs...lived a long time ago.**
> **All dinosaurs...lived in or near a swamp.**
> **All dinosaurs...were different sizes.**

Lesson 19

Jeanne Stone: *Cooperative Learning & Language Arts: A Multi-Structural Approach*
Kagan Publishing • 1 (800) 933-2667 • www.KaganOnline.com

When all the pages have been completed and reread, cut the book apart at the fold so that each page becomes a different strip. Using a pocket chart or tape on the back of each strip, post the strips so the students can reread them silently. Have the students think about which ideas go together and which idea might be first when writing about "All dinosaurs." As the students give you their ideas, begin to rearrange the strips in the order they suggest.

Show the students how these ideas can then be turned into sentences to complete a class report on "All dinosaurs."

5 Making Strip Books using *Team Project*

Assign the following roles to the students:

• #1 is the Recorder to write the responses

• #2 is the Reader who leads the rereading after every 5 entries in the strip book

• #3 is the Checker to see that the team agrees, checking for consensus, before a response is written

• #4 is the Cutter/Organizer who will cut the book when it is done and organize the strips for the group

Each team begins making two strip books — one about meat-eating dinosaurs (with a red marker) and the other about plant-eating dinosaurs (with a green marker). After each book is made, team member #4 cuts it apart.

 **Teacher's Note:** A Venn diagram is included for those that wish to introduce it at this time. As the students sort the strips, the different colored markers will guide them in using a Venn diagram.

Students organize the information they have by finding common characteristics of the two kinds of dinosaurs.

Meat-eating	Both	Plant-eating
eats meat	different sizes	eats plants
sharp teeth	lived long ago	flat teeth
lived on land	left fossils	lived in or near
sharp claws		water
walked on 2 legs		armor
		walked on 4 legs

6 Writing about dinosaurs using *Independent Writing*

Using the team's organized strips, each student begins writing about dinosaurs. Students can organize the information in one of two ways.

Example 1:

Paragraph 1 is about all dinosaurs.

Paragraph 2 is about meat-eating dinosaurs.

Paragraph 3 is about plant-eating dinosaurs.

In paragraphs 2 and 3, the characteristics about the specific kind of dinosaurs are listed in the same order in both paragraphs. For example, a paragraph about meat-eating dinosaurs might be about size, habitat, and food. The paragraph about plant-eating dinosaurs would then also be about size, habitat, and food.

Lesson 19

Example 2:

Paragraph 1 is about all dinosaurs.

Paragraph 2 is about a characteristic of both dinosaurs (habitat).

Paragraph 3 is about a different characteristic (body parts).

Paragraph 4 is about a different characteristic (food).

7 Responding to writing using *Three-Step Interview*

Working in interview pairs, students read their writing to each other. They respond to each other's writings by sharing about the accuracy of the information and the general impact that the writing has on them. During RoundRobin, the students summarize the writing that was read by their partners.

After the Three-Step Interview is completed, allow time for students to make any changes they wish. Comments and/or questions from team members may encourage students to make changes to improve their writing.

Teacher's Note: Before having your students do this part of the activity, make sure they have had an editing lesson that teaches them how to edit papers easily, successfully, and quickly.

8 Editing writing using *Simultaneous RoundTable*

If the students are ready to move beyond the content of the writing and work with each other on correctness, Simultaneous RoundTable is a quick way for team editing. Each round concentrates on a specific aspect of correctness.

Round #1 - Punctuation
Round #2 - Capitalization
Round #3 - Spelling
Round #4 - Sentence Structure

The team's papers are then passed around the team in Simultaneous RoundTable with each person checking each paper for the particular errors in that round. After four rounds, the RoundTable stops.

xtension

Across the Curriculum
Other science and social studies materials can easily be adapted to this format. Some sample topics might be:

Static and Current Electricity

Traveling to the West By Covered Wagon and By Ship

Planets and Stars

Neighborhood and City

Lesson 19

Jeanne Stone: *Cooperative Learning & Language Arts: A Multi-Structural Approach*
Kagan Publishing • 1 (800) 933-2667 • www.KaganOnline.com

212

Dinosaur Compare/Contrast

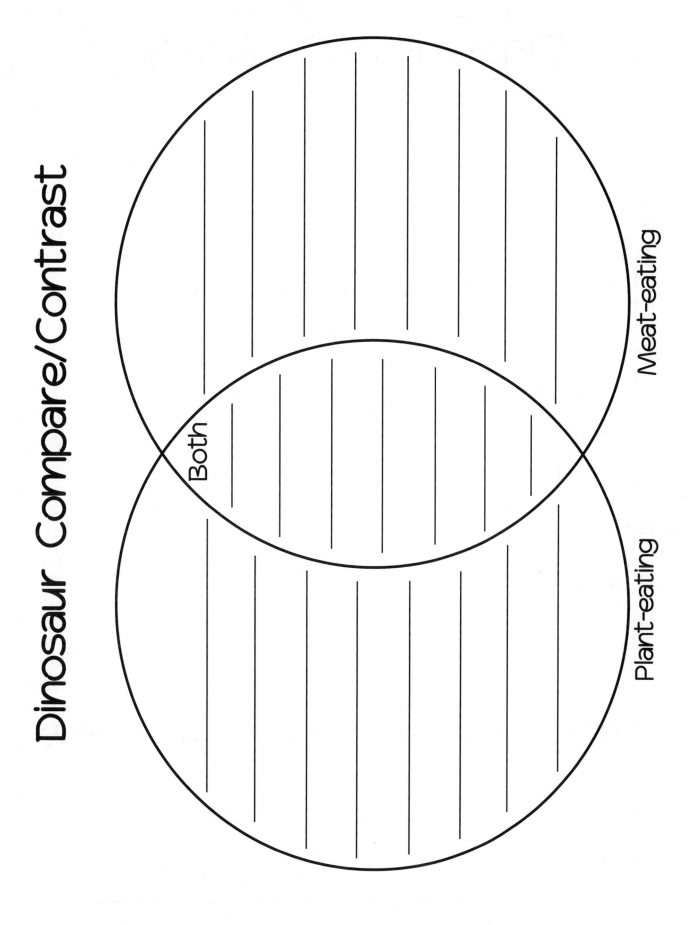

Meat-eating

Plant-eating

Both

Jeanne Stone: *Cooperative Learning & Language Arts: A Multi-Structural Approach*
Kagan Publishing • 1 (800) 933-2667 • www.KaganOnline.com

Dinosaur Note-Taking

Habitat

Body Description (size, covering, teeth, claws, etc.)

Food

Movement

Examples of _____ **dinosaurs**

Lesson 19

214

Jeanne Stone: *Cooperative Learning & Language Arts: A Multi-Structural Approach*
Kagan Publishing • 1 (800) 933-2667 • www.KaganOnline.com

Meat-Eating Dinosaurs

Meat-eating dinosaurs lived in a land that was warm and wet. It was swampy. There was water and land. The meat-eating dinosaurs stayed on the land all the time.

Most of the meat-eating dinosaurs walked and ran on their two hind legs. They usually had a stiff tail to help them balance. Their jaws were very strong. They had razor-sharp teeth.

The teeth were shaped like a triangle and often had rough edges. Their sharp claws were both weapons and knives. Some of the meat-eating dinosaurs were as small as a chicken and others were as big as a two-story house.

Meat-eating dinosaurs killed other dinosaurs. Some of them ate dead animals rather than attacking the larger plant-eating dinosaurs. Meat-eating dinosaurs killed with their teeth and their claws.

Some of the meat-eating dinosaurs are allosaurus, megalosaurus, deinonychus, and ceratosaurus. The king of the meat-eaters was tyrannosaurus rex. It was the largest but not the fastest meat-eater. The oviraptor ate the eggs of other dinosaurs.

Lesson 19

Plant-Eating Dinosaurs

Most of the dinosaurs were plant-eaters. They lived in or near the water so they could escape from the meat-eating dinosaurs. The largest plant-eaters stayed in the water almost all the time because it was easier for them to move.

Plant-eating dinosaurs had teeth like pegs so they could grind the plants they ate. Usually when the teeth wore down, new teeth would grow in. Some of the dinosaurs had weapons they could use against the meat-eating dinosaurs. The stegosaurus had body armor and spikes on its tail. The iguanodon had a spiky thumb that it used as a knife. The diplococus whipped its long tail around to stop its attacker.

Plant-eating dinosaurs had many plants to eat. Most plant-eating dinosaurs were large and ate all the time to get enough food. The smaller ones ate the ferns and grasses. The taller ones ate the bark and leaves off the bottom of trees. The tallest ones ate from the tops of the trees.

Another plant-eating dinosaur is the ankylosaur who had spikes running down each side of its body. The tip of its tail was a bony club. The proceratops was one of the smaller dinosaurs, only six feet long. The triceratops had three sharp horns on its head.

Jeanne Stone: *Cooperative Learning & Language Arts: A Multi-Structural Approach*
Kagan Publishing • 1 (800) 933-2667 • www.KaganOnline.com

Strip Books

Strip books are a great way to record students' ideas, create a book, and organize thoughts about a topic before writing.

1 Introduce a topic to the students and do some brainstorming.
"Tell me all the things you know about dinosaurs."

lived long ago	large	small
Brontosaurus	fierce	Tyrannosaurus Rex

2 Read a book about the topic (or provide material for the students to read).
"Today we will be learning about dinosaurs. Remember as many interesting things about dinosaurs as you can."

3 Record the ideas the students remember in a strip book. The first page is the title and the beginning of each sentences.

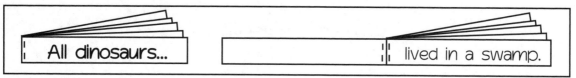

4 Read the book after every four or five ideas are added. Flip to the front to read the beginning of each sentence.

5 Separate the book. Put the pages in a pocket chart or tape them to the blackboard.

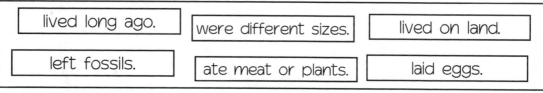

6 Discuss with the students the order they should be in. Move the strips as the students give suggestions.
"Which one would you like to begin with?" "What do dinosaurs look like?"
"What do they do?" "Which cards can be combined into one sentence?"

7 Have students write a paragraph from the sentences they have placed in order.

Lesson 19

Jeanne Stone: *Cooperative Learning & Language Arts: A Multi-Structural Approach*
Kagan Publishing • 1 (800) 933-2667 • www.KaganOnline.com

Brontosaurus

Jeanne Stone: *Cooperative Learning & Language Arts: A Multi-Structural Approach*
Kagan Publishing • 1 (800) 933-2667 • www.KaganOnline.com

Tyrannosaurus Rex

Jeanne Stone: *Cooperative Learning & Language Arts: A Multi-Structural Approach*
Kagan Publishing • 1 (800) 933-2667 • www.KaganOnline.com

Stegosaurus

Jeanne Stone: *Cooperative Learning & Language Arts: A Multi-Structural Approach*
Kagan Publishing • 1 (800) 933-2667 • www.KaganOnline.com

Ornithomimus

Jeanne Stone: *Cooperative Learning & Language Arts: A Multi-Structural Approach*
Kagan Publishing • 1 (800) 933-2667 • www.KaganOnline.com

What Bugs Me!

Grades 3 - 6

Lesson-At-A-Glance

Domain:
Imaginative/Narrative

Academic Skill:
Listening: Listen to others share
Speaking: Express a feeling
Reading: Identify a problem
Writing: Write to support a generalization with specific instances

Structures:
- *Three-Step Interview*
- *4S Brainstorming*
- *Think-Pair-Share*
- *Similarity Groups*
- *Pairs Square*
- *Fastwrite*
- *Team Discussion*
- *Teams Compare*
- *Independent Writing*
- *RoundRobin*

Materials:
- Small pieces of paper
- Chart paper cut in the shape of a trash can
- My Brother Bugs Me handout

Time:
2 or 3 language arts periods

Lesson Overview
Who doesn't like to complain? This lesson gives students an avenue to air those things that might "bug" them. Sharing orally and in writing, students express their feelings and give specific examples to support their feelings.

Lesson Sequence

1 Talking about what bugs you using *Three-Step Interview*

Students interview each other about things that bug them. Some examples might be: When my brother rides my bike. When a tall person sits in front of me at a show or movie and I can't see over his or her head. When I have to do my homework before I can play outside. Each student shares what bugs him or her, why it bugs them and when it usually happens. The students can tell about as many things as they want to.

Tell students that they are going to be writing about something that bugs them and why it bugs them.

2 Listing things that bug a person using *4S Brainstorming*

Assign the following roles to the students:
#1 Speed Captain: Encourages the team to work fast. Says things like, "Let's hurry!" "Let's get more ideas."

#2 Super Supporter: Encourages acceptance of all ideas with no evaluation. Says things like, "All ideas are great!" "Another fantastic idea!"

#3 Chief of Silly: Encourages silly ideas. Says things like, "Let's have a crazy idea."

#4 Synergy Guru: Encourages the team to build on each other's ideas. Says things like, "Let's combine those two." "Are there any more like that?"

With team member #1 as the recorder, the students brainstorm as many things as they can that bug them. These can be things at school, things at home, things with family, things with friends, things with people they don't know.

3 Picking one thing that bugs you using *Think-Pair-Share*

Students review the list that they brainstormed and select the one thing that bugs them the most. Tell the students to think of when it happens, who is usually involved and how it makes them feel. The students pair and share with a partner. Assure them it can be something different than they shared in the first interview. Select a few students who wish to share briefly with the class.

4 Finding others who dislike the same thing using *Similarity Groups*

Students write down what bugs them on a small piece of paper and then find others in the class with the same response. If there are a very wide variety of topics, you may want to suggest that they group by the person that bugs them: a parent, a friend, a classmate, a stranger, a brother, a sister, etc. Within their similarity groups, students pair up and discuss with each other what bugs them. Students repair and discuss again.

5 Forming new teams using *Pairs Square*

Each pair squares with another pair, forming a team of four. Students quickly RoundRobin their favorite T.V. show (or color, or sport, or cartoon character) as a teambuilding activity. Each new team of four finds a place to sit down together.

6 Sharing what bugs me using *Three-Step Interview*

Within the new teams, students interview each other about a specific time they were bugged. Encourage them to include the following information during the interview:

Who was involved?

What specifically happened?

When did it happen?

Where did it happen?

How did you feel?

7 Writing about what bugs you using *Fastwrite*

Have the students fastwrite for about ten minutes about the problem they discussed in the interview.

8 Identifying more descriptive writing using *Team Discussion*

Teacher's Note: When students write they usually make a list of generalizations rather than give detailed instances to support their generalization. One of the most important skills in writing is to support a generalization with specific instances.

Lesson 20

Show the students the following examples about "My brother bugs me." (See the handout at the end of this lesson.)

Example 1:

My brother bugs me.

Example 2:

It was 7:30 am and I was late already. I had misplaced my homework and wasted time looking for it. I was supposed to have walked to school with Bob and Tom, but they left without me. I hurried out to the garage to hop on my bike and race to school, but... That's right! Gone again! One of these days, I'm going to get the best of my brother instead of him getting the best of me.

In their teams, the students discuss what the difference is between the two examples. Some questions to prompt their discussion are:

Which tells what is happening?
Which shows what is happening?
Which is more interesting to read?
Which gives a better picture of how the boy feels?

Teacher's Note: The students can usually distinguish which paragraph is better and why. If not, have them close their eyes and visualize each group of sentences. The showing, descriptive paragraph gives them a clearer picture.

At the end of the discussion, have each team come up with a statement that summarizes their discussion.

9 **Exchanging answers with a neighboring team using** *Teams Compare*

Each team shares their statement with a team that is next to them. Ask for any common answers to be shared with the whole class.

10 **Writing about what bugs me using** *Independent Writing*

The students are then to write about what someone does to bug them by using specific descriptive examples. This can be an in-class activity or a homework assignment.

11 **Responding to writing using** *RoundRobin*

When the writing is completed, students share their writings in their teams. Each person reads his or her story to the whole team two times. (Individual copies can be passed out to each person if the students or teacher has had copies made.) Students listen so that they can point to the words and phrases that had an impact on them, summarize what they heard, and/or tell the writer how they felt when they were listening. Each student then, in RoundRobin fashion, comments on the writing. Examples of comments might be:

I liked the part when you said "..."
I could tell your sister really bugged you because "..."
The main point to me is...
I felt _____ when you read the story.

Lesson 20

xtensions

What Makes You _____?
Any emotion can be used in the blank. Use the lesson as it is, substituting the emotion for "What Bugs Me."

Holiday Tradition
Use this lesson as a frame to help the students write descriptive, showing remembrances of family holiday traditions.

Jeanne Stone: *Cooperative Learning & Language Arts: A Multi-Structural Approach*
Kagan Publishing • 1 (800) 933-2667 • www.KaganOnline.com

My Brother Bugs Me

Example 1:

My brother bugs me.

Example 2:

   It was 7:30 am and I was late already. I had misplaced my homework and wasted time looking for it.

I was supposed to have walked to school with Bob and Tom, but they left without me. I hurried out to the garage to hop on my bike and race to school, but… That's right! Gone again! One of these days, I'm going to get the best of my brother instead of him getting the best of me.

Jeanne Stone: *Cooperative Learning & Language Arts: A Multi-Structural Approach*
Kagan Publishing • 1 (800) 933-2667 • www.KaganOnline.com

Are You a Junk Food Junkie?

Grades 4 - 8

Lesson-At-A-Glance

Domain:
Analytical/Expository

Academic Skill:
Listening: Listen to others share
Speaking: Describe favorite snack food
Reading: Summarize what was read
Writing: Write a theme that rates three snack foods

Structures:
- *RoundRobin*
- *Teacher Talk*
- *Simultaneous RoundTable*
- *Numbered Heads Together*
- *4S Brainstorming*
- *Independent Writing*
- *Three-Step Interview*

Materials:
- Each student brings his/her favorite snack
- My Favorite Snacks handout
- 4 sheets paper per team - 1 each of blue, yellow, green red (pink)

Time:
1-2 language arts periods

Lesson Overview
Students love to eat, especially junk food like potato chips and candy bars. After describing their favorite snack food (junk or not), students will review the four food groups. They will then brainstorm a list of different snack foods. From this list they will choose three different snack foods and rate them as to their healthiness and how much they prefer to eat them.

Teacher's Note: A day or two before doing this lesson, ask the students to bring their favorite snack food to school on the day the lesson is planned.

Lesson Sequence

1 **Describing snack foods using** *RoundRobin*

On each team, students RoundRobin to describe the snack food they brought. The students should describe the snack and tell why they like eating it. Encourage students to go beyond "It's good."

2 Reviewing the four food groups using *Teacher Talk*

Review the four food groups (Meat, Milk, Fruits and Vegetables, and Breads and Cereals) with the students. Talk about what snacks are and how they should be part of a balanced diet.

3 Listing foods using *Simultaneous RoundTable*

Give each team four sheets of paper (one each of blue, yellow, green and pink). Each team member labels their papers as follows:

Team member #1: blue paper - Milk group

Team member #2: yellow paper - Breads and Cereals group

Team member #3: green paper - Fruits and Vegetables group

Team member #4: pink paper - Meat group

Using Simultaneous RoundTable, the teams pass the four papers around and record the appropriate foods on each sheet.

4 Reviewing the four food groups using *Numbered Heads Together*

Ask a variety of questions that review the four food groups and the part that snacks play in a balanced diet. For example, "Put your heads together and make sure everyone can name…

a snack that is a member of the Fruits and Vegetables group?"

a snack that is a member of the Milk group?"

a snack that is a member of the Meat group?"

a snack that is a member of the Breads and Cereals group?"

a good snack after you've had bacon and eggs, orange juice and milk for breakfast?"

5 Listing snacks using *4S Brainstorming*

Each team brainstorms snack foods that can be eaten — healthful snacks (members of the four food groups) or "junk food." When they finish, the foods on the list that are healthful should be marked in some way (an asterisk, underlined, or circled).

6 Describing snacks using *Simultaneous RoundTable*

Tell students that they will each choose three snack foods to rate based on their nutritional value and write a theme supporting their ratings.

Each student folds a blank paper into thirds horizontally. Have the students review the list of snack foods their group has and select three of them. At least one of the foods must be marked healthful. The students label each of the thirds on their papers with one of their chosen snack foods.

Using Simultaneous RoundTable, students pass around their papers and record a descriptive word or nutritional comment for any of the snack foods on the paper. By the end of the RoundTable, students should have at least four or five descriptors for each snack food.

Snickers

carrot

potato chips

Snickers
chewy
sweet
loads of sugar
carrot
crunchy
orange
full of vitamins
potato chips
oily
salty
crispy

Lesson 21

Jeanne Stone: *Cooperative Learning & Language Arts: A Multi-Structural Approach*
Kagan Publishing • 1 (800) 933-2667 • www.KaganOnline.com

The papers return to the students who started them. Each student cuts his or her sheet into thirds and places the three foods in order from the most healthful to the least healthful.

7 Writing to rate snacks using *Independent Writing*

Students write a five paragraph essay to support their ratings of the three snack foods they have chosen. The first paragraph introduces snack foods and tells what the student's three choices are. For example:

> Snack foods are between-meal treats. Some can be nutritious and some are not. Three snack foods I like are carrots, potato chips and a Snickers bar.

Paragraphs two through four each describe one of the snack foods in turn. Paragraph five concludes with a nutritional rating as well as a preferential rating. For example:

> Although I would rather eat a Snickers bar for a snack any day, carrots are the most nutritious snack I like to eat. Potato chips are not a very nutritious snack. For my snacking needs, I should eat carrots with an occasional Snickers or some potato chips thrown in.

 Teacher's Note: **My Favorite Snacks** handout is included if more student direction is necessary.

8 Responding to writing using *Three-Step Interview*

Working in interview pairs, students read their writings to each other. They respond to each other's writing by telling what their favorite part was and what general impact the content had on them. During the RoundRobin step, the students summarize their partner's writing. After the Three-Step Interview is completed, allow time for students to make any changes in their writings that they wish. Comments and questions from the other team members may encourage or help them in making changes to improve their writings.

9 Editing writing using *Simultaneous RoundTable*

If the students are ready to move beyond the content of the writing and work with each other on correctness, Simultaneous RoundTable is a quick way for team editing. During each round, the students concentrate on a specific area of correctness.

 Teacher's Note: Before having your students do this part of the lesson, make sure they have had an editing lesson that teaches them how to edit papers easily, successfully, and quickly. See Partner Editing in the Writing Structures Chapter.

Round #1: Punctuation
Round #2: Capitalization
Round #3: Spelling
Round #4: Sentence Structure

Lesson 21

The team's papers are passed around the team, just as in Simultaneous RoundTable, with each person checking each paper for the specific area of correctness in that round. After four rounds, the RoundTable stops.

xtensions

Vacation Spots
A similar lesson could be used to have students rate favorite vacation spots. The students could write for, or collect, travel brochures for a favorite vacation spot. The rating could be based on a variety of factors: cost, travel accessibility, and places of interest.

Music, Anyone?
Students could rate types of music or different radio stations (maybe doing a survey to find out what radio stations are listened to frequently).

Lesson 21

Jeanne Stone: *Cooperative Learning & Language Arts: A Multi-Structural Approach*
232   Kagan Publishing • 1 (800) 933-2667 • www.KaganOnline.com

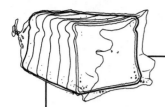

My Favorite Snacks

Snack foods are _____.

Some _____, but some_____.

My favorite snack foods are _____, _____,

and _____.

One of my favorite snacks is _____. I like to eat it because

_____. It is _____ and

especially _____. It's great for a snack because

_____.

Another snack I like to eat is _____. I like to eat it

because _____.

It is _____ and _____.

I always _____.

I also like to eat _____. It's _____

and _____. You can easily _____.

It's especially _____.

_____ is the most healthful snack I eat. I'd rather eat

_____ any day though. _____ is also a

_____ snack. For my snacking needs, I think I'll eat

_____ with an occasional _____

and _____ thrown in.

Lesson 21

Earthquake!

Grades 4 - 8

Lesson-At-A-Glance

Domain:
Analytical/Expository

Academic Skill:
    Writing: Write an essay

Structures:
- *Team Activity*
- *Three-Step Interview*
- *Team Discussion*
- *4S Brainstorming*
- *RoundRobin*
- *Independent Writing*

Materials:
- Books and encyclopedia articles about earthquakes
- 12 to 15 small pieces of paper per student

Time:
    1-2 language arts periods

Lesson Overview

Earthquakes (or any other natural disaster) can be devastating. In preparing for such an emergency, one needs to realize what things there are that are of intense sentimental value — things that cannot be replaced. This lesson allows students to talk and write about what things they would take with them if they have to evacuate quickly in case of a natural disaster.

Lesson Sequence

1 Feeling an "earthquake" using
Team Activity

Ask the students if they have ever felt an earthquake and tell them they will have a chance to experience a simulated one. Each team finds an open spot in the classroom (or move outside) and places one chair in the center with the team members standing around it. One team member sits in the chair while the others hold firmly onto the chair and rock it to simulate an earthquake. Each team member who wishes has a turn in the chair so that they all have a chance to feel the "earthquake."

The following roles may be assigned:

Team member #1 - Timer:
All students get 15 seconds of "earthquake"

Team member #2 - Monitor:
To make sure the chair does not get rocked too hard

Team member #3 - Gatekeeper:
To make sure all the team members have a turn

Team member #4 - Noise Monitor:
To make sure the noise level stays within the confines of the team

2 Telling about an experience using *Three-Step Interview*

Tell the students that they will be exploring their feelings about earthquakes and the damage that can occur. Have students use Three-Step Interview to share with each other about their experiences in an earthquake or other natural disaster.

3 Sharing information using *Team Discussion*

In their teams, students discuss everything they know about earthquakes. They may want to read and discuss additional information found in books or encyclopedia articles.

4 Listing valuable items using *4S Brainstorming*

Have the students think about what would happen if an earthquake were to damage their home and they had to leave. Using a separate piece of paper for each response, each team brainstorms the things they would take with them if they had to leave their houses in a hurry. When the brainstorming is completed, the team spreads out the responses where the whole team can see the responses. Each student reviews the responses and lists the four things that he or she would take with him or her. Students may choose the same item(s) if they wish.

5 Describing a valued item using *RoundRobin*

Now, the students each have four things that they would pack if they had to leave

home in a hurry. They will be writing essays that describe each of these things in detail and tell of their importance to the students.

Tell the students that they will each select one of their things to share with their team. Have them think about it in detail (drawing a picture of it may help some of the students). They will share a description of the object as well as its value to them. Team member #1 will start the RoundRobin which will continue until everyone has had a chance to share.

Teacher's Note: A RoundRobin can continue until the teammates have shared all four items or it can be stopped after one or two rounds.

(Optional)

5 Reviewing exclamation points using *Teacher Talk*

Because the topic of the writing draws out strong feelings, it may be appropriate to review the use of exclamation points to emphasize strong emotion.

6 Writing an essay using *Independent Writing*

Students write a multiple-paragraph essay about the four things they value and would not want to lose in an earthquake (or other disaster). In each paragraph, an item should be described in detail and its importance to the student given.

Lesson 22

A sample essay outline could be:
Paragraph 1: Introduce the circumstance and list the four items.

Paragraph 2-5: Tell about each item individually.

Paragraph 6: State the emotions involved with the choices.

xtensions

Three-Step Interview
Have students share their writing with their partners. The partners can ask questions about any parts that may need clarification in the essay. During the RoundRobin in Step 3, have the student share what they learned about their partner from the things that they would pack, rather than just summarizing what they heard.

After the RoundRobin, the students should be given an opportunity to revise.

Blast Off!
Use the same lesson format and have the students list and write about the four things they would take with them in a space shuttle.

Lesson 22

Jeanne Stone: *Cooperative Learning & Language Arts: A Multi-Structural Approach*
Kagan Publishing • 1 (800) 933-2667 • www.KaganOnline.com

237

To Whom It May Concern

Grades 5 - 8

Lesson-At-A-Glance

Domain:
Analytical/Expository

Academic Skill:

Listening: Listen in order to ask questions

Speaking: Participate in a role play

Reading: Draw conclusions
Make inferences

Writing: Write a persuasive letter
Write from another point of view

Structures:
- *4S Brainstorming*
- *Think-Pair-Share*
- *Three-Step Interview*
- *Fastwrite*
- *Team Interview*
- *Think-Write-Pair-Share*
- *Independent Writing*

Materials:
- Large pieces of paper (2 1/2" x 8 1/2")
- Chart paper
- I Think…handout

Time:
2 or 3 language arts periods

Lesson Overview

This lesson takes a student's knowledge of the Civil War (or any other historical period) and applies it in a new situation. Through a role-play interview and a fastwrite in character, students begin to see another person's point of view. This point of view is translated into letter form as each student writes to Mr. Lincoln from the point of view of someone involved in the Civil War.

This lesson can serve as a frame for a multi-structural lesson identifying another person's point of view, and writing a letter from that point of view. Although the specific example in this lesson is the Civil War — President Lincoln, any historical period and figure can be substituted. A prerequisite to this lesson, or any version of it with a different focus, is a thorough knowledge of the historical period being used.

This lesson can be removed from a social science context and be adapted to holidays such as Halloween (Dear Dracula) or Christmas (Dear Santa Claus) or life as it is today (Dear Principal or Dear Mom).

Lesson Sequence

1 Listing people using *4S Brainstorming*

Tell the students to think about the Civil War as they have studied it through films, novels, and reference materials. Have them think about all the people that were affected by the war and were aware of it. For example: a slave, a plantation owner, an abolitionist, a member of the underground railroad, and an eighteen year-old boy.

Assign the following roles to the students:

#1: Speed Captain - Encourages the team to work fast. Says things like, "Let's hurry!" "Let's get more ideas."

#2: Super Supporter - Encourages acceptance of all ideas with no evaluation. Says things like, "All ideas are great!" "Another fantastic idea!"

#3: Chief of Silly - Encourages silly ideas. Says things like, "Let's have a crazy idea."

#4: Synergy Guru - Encourages the team to build on each other's ideas. Says things like, "Let's combine those two." "Are there any more like that?"

With team member #2 as the recorder, the students brainstorm people that were affected by the Civil War. Have them record each person on a separate piece of paper, written large enough to read from a distance.

Post a class chart <u>People of the Civil War Era</u>. As students complete their brainstorming, have them select three or four people to tape or glue on the class chart.

2 Selecting a role using *Think-Pair-Share*

The students review the class list and think about who they would be if they were living during the Civil War. Have them pair up and share. Do a quick whip to share the variety of responses in the classroom.

3 Interviewing in role using *Three-Step Interview*

The students interview each other about the person they would have been if they had lived during the Civil War. Have them share such things as:

• Where would they be?
• What kinds of things would they be doing?
• Who would they associate with as coworkers? As friends?
• How would they feel?

During RoundRobin, encourage the students to share as if they are sharing about someone they knew during the Civil War.

4 Writing within their role using *Fastwrite*

Students write for fifteen minutes describing who they are, where they are, the feelings they have, and the kinds of things they are doing. Remind them to include their feelings about the war and its impact on them.

5 Responding to writing using *Team Interview*

Team member #1 sits in the middle of each team and reads his or her fastwrite to the team to acquaint them with who they are. After listening to the fastwrite, the other team members interview them in their roles.

Lesson 23

Repeat the process until all the team members have been interviewed in role.

6 Expressing concerns using *Think-Write-Pair-Share*

Explain to the students that now that they have a new identity, they are going to write a letter to President Lincoln expressing a concern they have about the Civil War. Students think of concerns they, in their new identity, would have and briefly write a series of sentences expressing these concerns on the **I Think...** handout.

> I think...
>
> I feel...
>
> I hate...
>
> I need...
>
> I want...
>
> I like...

Each student reviews his or her list and selects a major concern. Have the students pair up and discuss their concern. Encourage them to go beyond just stating I think...and to include some reasons why this is a major concern that needs to be brought to the attention of President Lincoln. Ask for some students to share their statements with the class.

7 Writing a letter using *Independent Writing*

The students write letters to President Lincoln expressing their concerns, and trying to persuade President Lincoln to act to resolve the concern.

8 Responding to writing using *Team Interview*

One member of each team sits in the middle of the team. That member reads

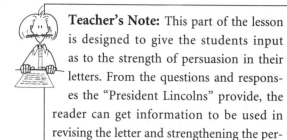

Teacher's Note: This part of the lesson is designed to give the students input as to the strength of persuasion in their letters. From the questions and responses the "President Lincolns" provide, the reader can get information to be used in revising the letter and strengthening the persuasion in it.

his or her letter. The other team members, acting as President Lincoln, respond to the reader.

The process continues until all students have read their letters and had responses from the "President Lincolns."

Allow students time to revise their letters.

Extensions

From President Lincoln
The students trade letters. Ask them to write a response to the letter as if they were President Lincoln. In the response, they should portray President Lincoln's feelings about the concerns and any actions, if any, that they as President Lincoln may take.

Dear Fellow Citizens
All students pretend they are President Lincoln. Have them write a letter that President Lincoln would send to the nation after the Civil War, to begin the process of reunification.

Lesson 23

I Think...

I Think_____

_____

_____

I feel_____

_____

_____

I hate_____

_____

_____

I want_____

_____

_____

I need_____

_____

_____

I like_____

_____

_____

Jeanne Stone: *Cooperative Learning & Language Arts: A Multi-Structural Approach*
Kagan Publishing • 1 (800) 933-2667 • www.KaganOnline.com

Bibliography

Children's Books

Aesop. *Aesop's Fables* (edited by Ann McGovern). Scholastic, Inc.

Aesop. *Aesop's Fables* (selected and illustrated by Michael Hague). Holt, Rinehart and Winston, 1985.

Alcott, Louisa May. *Little Women.* Little, Brown, 1868.

Alexander, Martha. *Nobody Ever Asked Me If I Wanted a Baby Sister.* Dial, 1971.

Anderson, Hans Christian. *The Emperor's New Clothes.* Harper & Row, 1982.

Barrett, Judi. *Animals Should Definitely Not Wear Clothing.* Atheneum, 1970.

Barrie, J. M. *Peter Pan.* Viking, 1911.

Baylor, Byrd. *Plink, Plink, Plink.* Houghton, 1971.

Beskow, Elsa. *Pele's New Suit.*

Blegvad, Lenore. *Anna Banana and Me.* McElderberry, 1985.

Bond, Michael. *A Bear Called Paddington.* Houghton Mifflin, 1960.

Borten, Helken. *Do You Hear What I Hear?* Abelard-Schuman, 1960.

Brown, Margaret Wise. *The City Noisy Book.* Harper & Row, 1940.

Brown, Margaret Wise. *The Indoor Noisy Book.* Harper & Row, 1942.

Brown, Margaret Wise. *The Noisy Book.* Harper & Row, 1947.

Brown, Margaret Wise. *The Winter Noisy Book.* Harper & Row, 1947.

Bunting, Eve. *Valentine Bears.* Houghton Mifflin, 1983.

Burnett, Frances Hodgson. *The Secret Garden.* Lippincott, 1912.

Byars, Betsy. *The Pinballs.* Harper & Row, 1977.

Jeanne Stone: *Cooperative Learning & Language Arts: A Multi-Structural Approach*
Kagan Publishing • 1 (800) 933-2667 • www.KaganOnline.com

243

Carle, Eric. *Do You Want to Be My Friend?* Crowell, 1971.

Carle, Eric. *The Honeybee and the Robber.* Philomel, 1981.

Carle, Eric. *The Very Busy Spider.* Philomel, 1985.

Cleaver, Vera and Bill. *Where the Lilies Bloom.* Lippincott, 1969.

Cohen, Miriam. *Will I Have a Friend?* Macmillan, 1967.

Dahl, Roald. *Boy: Tales of Childhood.* Farrar, Strauss, 1984.

de Paola, Tomie. *Charlie Needs a Cloak.* Simon and Schuster, 1973.

de Paola, Tomie. *Pancakes for Breakfast.* Harcourt, 1978.

de Paola, Tomie. *The Popcorn Book.* Holiday House, 1978.

de Regniers, Beatrice Schenk. *May I Bring A Friend?* Atheneum, 1964.

de Regniers, Beatrice Schenk. *What Can You Do With a Shoe?* Harper & Row, 1955.

de Trevino, Elizabeth Borton. *I, Juan de Pareja.* Farrar, Strauss, 1965.

Ehlert, Lois. *Growing Vegetable Soup.* Harcourt Brace Jovanovich, 1987.

Estes, Eleanor. *The Hundred Dresses.* Harcourt Brace Jovanovich, 1944.

Fatio, Louise. *The Happy Lion and the Bear.* McGraw Hill, 1964.

Fitzhugh, Louise. *Harriet the Spy.* Harper & Row, 1964.

Flack, Marjorie. *Ask Mr. Bear.* Macmillan, 1932.

Frank, Anne. *The Diary of Anne Frank.* Doubleday, 1967.

Freeman, Don. *Corduroy.* Viking, 1968.

Freeman, Don. *A Rainbow of My Own.* Viking, 1966.

Fritz, Jean. *Homesick: My Own Story.* Putnam, 1982.

Galdone, Paul. *The Gingerbread Boy.* Houghton Mifflin, 1975.

Galdone, Paul. *Jack and the Beanstalk.* Houghton Mifflin, 1974.

Galdone, Paul. *Three Aesop Fox Tales.* Houghton Mifflin, 1971.

Galdone, Paul. *Three Billy Goats Gruff.* Houghton Mifflin, 1973.

Gardiner, John R. *Stone Fox.* Crowell, 1980.

Garelick, May. *Sounds of a Summer Night.* Addison-Wesley, 1963.

George, Jean. *My Side of the Mountain.* Dutton, 1959.

Heide, Florence P. *Sounds of Sunshine, Sounds of Rain.* Parents, 1970.

Hoban, Russell. *A Baby Sister for Frances.* Scholastic, 1976.

Hoban, Russell. *Bread and Jam for Frances.* Harper & Row, 1964.

Hopkins, Lee. *Best Friends.* Harper & Row, 1986.

Jacobs, Joseph, editor. "Tattercoats" in *More English Fairy Tales.* Amereon Ltd.

Kalen, Robert. *Rain.* Greenwillow, 1978.

Keats, Ezra Jack. *Peter's Chair.* Harper & Row, 1967.

Kaufman, Lois. *What's That Noise?* Lothrop, 1965.

Keller, Helen. *The Story of My Life.* Doubleday, 1954.

Kellogg, Steven. *Best Friends.* Dial, 1985.

Lawson, Robert. *Ben and Me.* Little, Brown, 1939.

Lionni, Leo. *Frederick's Fables.* Pantheon, 1985.

Lobel, Arnold. *Frog and Toad Are Friends.* Harper & Row, 1970. *Fables.* Harper & Row, 1980.

Lord, Betty Bao. *In the Year of the Boar and Jackie Robinson.* Harper & Row, 1984.

Louie, Ai-ling. *Yeh-Shen.* Philomel, 1982.

Lovelace, Maud Hart. *Besty Tacy.* Harper & Row, 1940.

McCloskey, Robert. *Blueberries for Sal.* Viking, 1948.

McCloskey, Robert. *Homer Price.* Viking, 1943.

Part IV

Martin, Bill. *Listen to the Rain.* Henry Holt & Co., 1988.

Marshall, James. *George and Martha.* Houghton, 1972.

Mayer, Mercer. *A Boy, a Dog, and a Frog.* Dial, 1967.

Miller, Edna. *Mousekin's Fables.* Prentice Hall, 1985.

Milne, E. B. *Winnie the Pooh.* Dutton, 1926.

Minarik, Else Holmelund. *Little Bear.* Harper & Row, 1957.

Morey, Walt. *Gentle Ben.* Dutton, 1965.

Numeroff, Laura Joffe. *If You Give a Mouse a Cookie.* Harper & Row, 1985.

O'Dell, Scott. *Island of the Blue Dolphins.* Houghton Mifflin, 1960.

O'Dell, Scott. *Zia.* Dell, 1978

Paterson, Katherine. *Bridge to Terebitha.* Crowell, 1977.

Peek, Merle. *Mary Wore Her Red Dress and Henry Wore His Green Sneakers.* Clarion, 1985.

Peet, Bill. *Big Bad Bruce.* Houghton Mifflin, 1977.

Perrault, Charles. *Cinderella* retold by Amy Ehrlich. Dial, 1985.

Petty, Kate and Lisa Kopper. *What's That Taste?* Franklin Watts, 1986.

Piper, Watty. *The Little Engine That Could.* Platt & Munk, 1930.

Pluckrose, Henry. *Think About Tasting.* Franklin Watts, 1986.

Ruis, Maria. *Hearing.* Barron's Educational Service, 1985.

Ruis, Maria. *Taste.* Barron's Educational Service, 1985.

Sawyer, Ruth. *Journey Cake, Ho!* Viking, 1953.

Sendak, Maurice. *Where the Wild Things Are.* Harper & Row,1962.

Serfozo, Mary. *Who Said Red?* McElderry Books, 1988.

Seuss, Dr. *The 500 Hats of Bartholomew Cubbins.* Vanguard.

Seuss, Dr. *Green Eggs and Ham.* Beginner Books, 1960.

Showers, Paul. *The Listening Walk.* Crowell, 1961.

Slobodkina, Esphyr. *Caps for Sale.* Addison-Wesley, 1947.

Spier, Peter. *Crash, Bang, Boom.* Doubleday, 1972.

Spier, Peter. *Gobble, Growl, and Grunt.* Doubleday, 1971.

Steig, William. *Amos and Boris.* Farrar, Straus, 1971.

Steiner, Charlotte. *Listen to My Seashell.* Knopf, 1959.

Stevenson, James. *Worse Than Willy!* Greenwillow, 1984.

Stinson, Kathy. *Red is Best.* Annick Press Ltd., 1982.

Taylor, Sydney. *All-of-a-Kind-Family.* Yearling, 1951.

Tressalt, Alvin. *The Mitten.* Scholastic, 1964.

Turkle, Brinton. *Deep in the Forest.* E. P. Dutton, 1976.

Vincent, Gabrielle. *Ernest and Celestine.* Greenwillow, 1982.

Viorst, Judith. *Alexander and the Terrible, Horrible, No Good, Very Bad Day.* Atheneum, 1972.

Viorst, Judith. *I'll Fix Anthony.* Harper, 1969.

Viorst, Judith. *Tales of a Fourth Grade Nothing.* Dutton, 1972.

Waber, Bernard. *Ira Sleeps Over.* Houghton Mifflin, 1972.

Ward, Lynd. *The Biggest Bear.* Houghton, Mifflin, 1952.

White, E. B. *Charlotte's Web.* Harper & Row, 1952.

Wilder, Laura Ingalls. *The Little House in the Big Woods.* Harper & Row, 1953.

Wilder, Laura Ingalls. *Little House on the Prairie.* Harper & Row, 1986

Winthrop, Elizabeth. *Shoes.* Harper & Row, 1986.

Part IV

Wiseman, Bernard. *Morris and Boris.* Dodd, 1974.

Ziefert, Harriet. *A New Coat for Anna.* Knopf, 1986.

Zion, Gene. *Harry and the Lady Next Door.* Harper & Row, 1960.

Zolotow, Charlotte. *Big Sister and Little Sister.* Harper & Row, 1966.

Zolotow, Charlotte. *The Hating Book.* Harper & Row, 1969.

Zolotow, Charlotte. *Mr. Rabbit and the Lovely Present.* Harper & Row, 1962.

Poetry Anthologies

dePaola, Tomie. *Tomie dePaola's Mother Goose.* Putnam, 1985.

O'Neill, Mary. *Hailstones and Halibut Bones.* Doubleday & Co., 1961.

Prelutsky, Jack. *The New Kid on the Block.* Greenwillow, 1984.

Prelutsky, Jack, editor. *The Random House Book of Poetry for Children.* Random House, 1983.

Prelutsky, Jack, *Read Aloud Rhymes for the Very Young.* Knopf, 1986.

Silverstein, Shel. *A Light in the Attic.* Harper & Row, 1981.

Silverstein, Shel. *Where the Sidewalk Ends.* Harper & Row, 1974.

Teacher's Resources

Children's Literature in the Reading Program. Edited by Bernice E. Cullinan. International Reading Association, 1987.

English-Language Arts Framework. California State Department of Education, 1987.

English-Language Arts Model Curriculum Guide. California State Department of Education, 1988.

Frank, Marjorie. *If You're Trying to Teach Kids How to Write, You've Gotta Have This Book.* Incentive Publications, 1979.

Handbook for Planning an Effective Literature Program. California State Department of Education, 1987.

Handbook for Planning an Effective Writing Program. California State Department of Education, 1986.

Olsen, Mary Lou. *Creative Connections.* Libraries Unlimited, Inc., 1987.

Practical Ideas for Teaching Writing as a Process. Edited by Carol Booth Olson. California State Department of Education, 1986.

Recommended Readings in Literature. California State Department of Education, 1986.

Schaff, Joanne. *The Language Arts Idea Book.* Scott, Foresman and Company, 1976.

Part IV

Jeanne Stone: *Cooperative Learning & Language Arts: A Multi-Structural Approach*
Kagan Publishing • 1 (800) 933-2667 • www.KaganOnline.com

246

Notes

Notes

Notes

Notes